CONSIDER JESUS

CONSIDER JESUS

Waves of Renewal in Christology

Elizabeth A. Johnson

CROSSROAD · NEW YORK

In Memoriam
Virginia Therese Callahan, C.S.J.
(1920–1985)
A woman of courage and joy
who always encouraged questions.

This Printing: 2003

The Crossroad Publishing Company
370 Lexington Avenue, New York, N.Y. 10017

Printed in the United States of America

Library of Congress Cataloging-in-Publication Data

Johnson, Elizabeth A., 1941–
  Consider Jesus : waves of renewal in christology / Elizabeth A.
Johnson.
    p. cm.
  Includes bibliographical references.
  ISBN 0-8245-0990-0; 0-8245-1161-1 (pbk.)
  1. Jesus Christ—History of doctrines—20th century. 2. Catholic
Church—Doctrines—20th century. I. Title.
BT198.J635 1990
232'.09'045—dc20   89-37282
                                                          CIP

Grateful acknowledgment is made to *Chicago Studies* for permis-
sion to reprint "Christology and Social Justice: John Paul II and the
American Bishops," which appeared in vol. 26 (1987), pp. 155–65.

Contents

Preface

The chapters in this book originally saw the light of day as lectures. Their first purpose was to present the fundamental rethinking taking place in christology to persons who are actively involved in ministries in the church or who are seeking greater understanding of their faith. Given the vital interests of this audience the lectures took on a certain character, seeking to inform about the reams of scholarship pouring forth about Jesus Christ in order to open doors for more effective preaching, teaching, prayer, and pastoral action. It has always been my conviction that nothing inspires a life of vital, active faith so powerfully as an occasional dose of good thinking about the faith, which we call theology. At least it is one of the most effective sources of what the scriptures call *paraklesis,* or mutual encouragement, and the direction that it can give to effective ministry over the long haul of a lifetime is profound. Cycling these lectures into book form is being done with the conviction that a wider circle of thoughtful believers will find benefit for their lives and ministry in pondering recent theological insights into Jesus Christ.

It will be noticed that the approach to the subject is taken largely through Catholic authors. At mid-twentieth century when the renewal in Catholic christology can be said to have begun, Catholic unlike Protestant thought was heavily entrenched in an approach to Jesus Christ through dogma and had remained virtually unscathed by the roiling debates over biblical matters that so influenced Protestant christology. In addition, fundamental differences in theological anthropology continue to characterize these two streams of Christianity. Thus Catholics started into the renewal process with a different problematic, and have continued with a different set of basic assumptions about the relation of God to human beings, especially when it comes to the saving work of Christ. Catholic christology therefore has a distinct tone or flavor, and its story needs to be told in its own way. This is not to say, however, that insights into Christ are restricted to the Catholic community. Far from it! In this area Protestant scholarship has been outstanding as names such as Barth, Bultmann, Moltmann, and Pannenberg suggest. In present ecumenical times, theological influence has flown more freely back and forth across the division of the churches. This good state of affairs is reflected in the later chapters of this book which recount more recent christological developments.

I have chosen the metaphor of waves breaking on the beach to unify this vast body of material. As a wave is created by wind at sea and then rises up, rolls in, and breaks as it comes close to land, so too it seems that successive understandings of Christ have formed, swelled, and broken upon Catholic consciousness since the mid-twentieth century. The first wave in the 1950's consisted in remembering the genuine humanity of Jesus Christ, a memory stirred up by the 1,500th anniversary of the ancient council of Chalcedon which had declared the christological dogma. A decade later biblical scholarship began to flourish, triggering critical discovery of the history of Jesus. Both of these waves overlapped as they arrived in a church that was incorporating concern for justice into its sense of mission. Before they had time to recede, a third wave formed as the voice of the poor began to be heard doing theology from the "underside of history" and so claiming

Jesus Christ as liberator. Almost simultaneously the movement of feminist theology stirred yet another wave to life,
swelling as the majority of the church's members who had
long been left out of the conversation about Christ began to
articulate their insights. Even more recently a realization of
the vastness of the world and its peoples has arisen, and looms
as a question about the universal influence of Jesus the Christ.
Under threat of ecological disaster, global vision now grows
even wider to incorporate the view that not only human
beings but all creatures of the earth and the universe itself are
destined for final blessing in Christ. Thus pressures, needs,
and new scholarship both inside the church and in the wider,
tightly knit, anguished world have conspired together to
create wave after wave of new insight into Jesus Christ. As with
all waves, these are not always clearly separated from one
another; as waves will do, they are collectively changing the
shape of the landscape.

This last half-century of development in christology brings
into clear view the fact that the Christian community is borne
by a living tradition. As a vital, creative movement in time,
this tradition hands on its inherited truth enriched through
living response to new experiences. The witness of generations who have believed before us has brought the church to
this moment in its pilgrimage. In turn, adult believers now
have the responsibility to utter their own christological word,
personally and collectively as church, so that faith in Jesus
Christ may be passed on to the next generation in a truly
living state. These chapters have been written toward that end.

I would like to express warm appreciation to those who
first invited me to present these lectures: the Program for
Ministry to Priests of the Archdiocese of Seattle, Washington,
and of the Diocese of Richmond, Virginia; the Lay Ministry
Formation Program of the Archdiocese of Baltimore; the
Probe Workshop organized by the Paulist Center in the Arch-

diocese of Toronto, Canada; the Institute of Spirituality sponsored by the Sisters of St. Joseph, Brentwood, New York; and the Ongoing Formation Program in Ponce, Puerto Rico.

In a special way my heartfelt thanks goes to the Theological Winter School sponsored by the South African Catholic Bishops Conference who invited me to present these lectures on tour throughout their country and saw to it that these lectures were first published. The present book is an outgrowth of that South African publication, entitled *Who Do You Say That I Am? Introducing Contemporary Christology* and published by the Order of Preachers at Hilton. This version differs from the first by the addition of bibliography for each chapter, and by the inclusion of chapter five with its American references.

I am grateful to all who participated in these lectures whether in situations of relative peace and prosperity or situations of violence and oppression. We thought aloud together about the significance of Jesus Christ, and it is in such mutual give and take that insights are truly born. A final word of gratitude goes to editor Frank Oveis, who in a serendipitous moment discovered these lectures in their South African form and saw their possibility for a North American public.

Surrounded by a cloud of witnesses, we set ourselves to the task of faith to "consider Jesus" (Heb 3:1).

1

A Living Tradition

A seed grows into a flowering tree. A glimmer of an idea matures into full-fledged insight. A young lover discovers ever greater depths in the beloved one, none of which can be fully expressed in words although loving words when spoken do deepen the relationship. A new interpretation of a law brings more of its original richness to light. Each of these experiences has been used to illumine the development of doctrine, that change in the Christian intellectual heritage that happens when followers of Jesus Christ live out their faith in new situations. Through prayer and thought in the context of new initiatives and responses given by the community of believers, insights develop. Different ways of expressing the meaning of faith in accord with cultural variations develop. Doctrine develops. Whether the image be taken from the world of nature, from human psychology, or from the social order, the analogies of the tree, the lover, and the interpretation of law suggest something alive in history. They point to a vital community of faith nourishing not a dead but a living tradition.

This is not to suggest that doctrinal development is a triumphant march of progress along a straight line from truth to truth. The historical record shows otherwise, indicating detours, U-turns, and plain forgetfulness in the community's appropriation of its heritage. But it is to put clearly in the spotlight the fact that guided by the Spirit of God Christian

1

believers throughout two thousand years have never stopped
expressing their faith in Jesus Christ, their affection for him,
and their understanding of his significance in words and
deeds coherent with their time and place. The ongoing story
of this community thus involves two elements, the old with
the new, or the historically given with its current form of
reception.

At the start of an essay on education, the Jewish religious
thinker Martin Buber wrote these engaging lines which give
us yet another analogy for our situation as a community with
a living tradition:

> In every hour the human race begins. We forget this too easily
> in face of the massive fact of past life, of so-called world history,
> of the fact that each child is born with a given disposition of
> world historical origin, that is, inherited from the riches of the
> whole human race, and also born into a given situation of
> world historical origin, that is, produced from the riches of the
> world's events. This fact must not obscure the other no less
> important fact that in spite of everything, in this as in every
> hour, what has not been invades the structure of what is, with
> ten thousand countenances, of which not one has been seen
> before, with ten thousand souls still undeveloped but ready to
> develop—a creative event if ever there was one, newness rising
> up, primal potential might. This potentiality, streaming uncon-
> quered, however much of it is squandered, is the reality *child:*
> this phenomenon of uniqueness, which is more than just
> begetting and birth, this grace of beginning again and ever
> again.*

In this passionate description of the creative potential of new
human beings the importance of both the old and the new are
highlighted. Each child receives from the riches of the world

---

*Martin Buber, "Education," *Between Man and Man* (New York: Macmillan, 1966), 83.

while at the same time he or she brings to the world something never before seen. As a community with a living tradition Christians find themselves similarly gifted. Believers today receive an enormously rich heritage woven by the
struggles and advances of the cloud of witnesses that has gone
before, at the same time that they must witness to the good
news in ways that are credible to their own world and to their
own heart. If it is not to stagnate and dry out a living tradition
needs to be passed on in a living condition.

All of this serves to introduce that theology which reflects
on the meaning of Jesus Christ. For here in the first Christian
centuries is a striking example of the development of doctrine
in a living church. Here too is ferment in Catholic theology
today which signals that the development is not over yet. One
way often used to focus this issue is to pose the question about
Jesus as Jesus himself does in the synoptic gospels. In Mark's
narration:

> And Jesus went on with his disciples to the villages of Casarea
> Philippi; and on the way he asked his disciples, "Who do
> people say that I am?" And they told him, "Some say John the
> Baptist, and others say Elijah, and still others say one of the
> prophets." And he asked them, "But who do *you* say that I
> am?" (Mk 8:27–29)

Most Christians know Peter's answer—you are the Christ (v.
29); and Martha's answer—you are the Christ, the Son of
God, the one who is coming into the world (Jn 11:27); and
the answers of the first generations of disciples whose insights
frame the scriptural testimony. But the question does not rest
there, with these answers. It resounds through the centuries
inviting a response from every generation of believers and
from every disciple. Who do you say that I am? The question
is not the only way of framing the issue of Jesus' significance
and, as we will see, there are some occasions when it may not

be the best way. But it is a good question, one which sets us to thinking both personally and corporately.

The question itself is not academic but arises from the experience of salvation. Something exceedingly good happens to people in their encounter with Jesus Christ. Fundamentally they are put right with God. Consequently they come to themselves, being restored to inner integrity, healed in body and spirit. Relationships with other people are also healed and peace becomes a real possibility. People experience a new lease on life pervaded with hope in the future, even if it be hope against hope. Among those who have been thus graced by the Spirit of Christ, community forms. Given the profound impact of Jesus Christ on their lives the question naturally arises—who is he? The experience of salvation coming from God in Jesus makes him fundamentally interesting.

The answer to this question has not been academic either. In personal faith and piety, in official doctrine, in liturgy, and in the way people actually live the answer is always a matter of faith. As the faith of a pilgrim people is always historically inculturated, disciples of every generation have answered the question in thought patterns and images familiar to them from their particular cultures. The whole church as well utters its christological answer in every age as an ecclesial act. Each of us who believes today has been shaped by the answers of our ancestors in the faith. As the inheritors of two thousand years of a living tradition we are like "pygmies on the shoulders of giants," able to see far thanks to the stature of those who have handed on the tradition to us. Now it is our turn. Our times face new crises, demands, and critical challenges, and the meaning of Jesus Christ is being sharpened once again in engagement with needs in diverse quarters of the world. As baptized persons graced by the Holy Spirit dwelling within us, each of us is called to utter our own personal christological answer by word and deed; so too the church as a whole, in the idiom of our age. We do not do so out of whole cloth, however, but faithful to the truth handed on by the living tradition. A brief walk through history will highlight what our ancestors in the faith have bequeathed to us by way of answers to the christological question, and will point to factors in the world that have occasioned new ferment in the ongoing process of answering it.

1. Biblical Christology (First Century A.D.)

It began with an encounter, as first-century Jewish women and men came in contact with the itinerant preacher Jesus of Nazareth, himself Jewish. He was hailed as a prophet mighty in word and deed. His preaching emphasized that salvation is on its way from God; in other words, that God is on the side of the little ones, the outcast, even the sinners, promising them new life. In light of the coming salvation, all persons, whatever their status, are called to conversion. All are called to open their hearts to receive the mercy of God. For the powerful, this involves a turn of heart and mind toward their brothers and sisters.

Jesus took this good news which he preached in spoken parables and enacted it in living parables. His table fellowship with sinners, his healing people of suffering in spirit and body, and his bold reproach to repressive authorities held out the promise of life to all in concrete ways. Around him gathered women and men called to be his disciples, following his way and sharing his efforts on behalf of the reign of God.

In a short time he was rejected by most religious leaders of his own faith. Arrested and tortured in prison, he was publicly executed by the civil authorities. After his death his mourning disciples experienced him as alive in a new way. God had raised him up! Present through the power of the Holy Spirit, he continues to be the one through whom the compassionate love of God is poured out upon the world to heal grief and alienation and to overcome sin and even death.

The disciples experienced salvation coming from God through him, with ramifications in every dimension of their lives. They preached the good news and suffered for it, expressing his significance in their lives by proclaiming his story as the story of the living one. Since the earliest disciples were Jews they turned to their own scriptures for help in interpreting him. There they found the divine promise embedded in such figures as the Messiah, Son of Man, Suffering Servant, Wisdom, Son of God, and so on. They used these evocative symbols to explain Jesus Christ's meaning and even turned some of them into titles for him. When they did this, his own life history and especially the cross revised what the symbols themselves meant. For example, no longer was Messiah the simply triumphant king of the Davidic line, but the crucified and risen one.

By the second and third decade after the crucifixion, communities of believers had formed all over the Mediterranean world. These reflected different characteristics coherent with their diverse cultural and sociological settings (Jewish or Gentile, persecuted or at peace, provincial or cosmopolitan). Certain of their members took up their quills to write their understandings of Jesus with insights shaped by the preaching and other experiences of their local churches. What resulted was a nuanced diversity of responses to the basic question: Who do you say that I am? Some of the key answers include:

Paul—Jesus is the crucified and risen Christ

Mark—Jesus is the suffering Messiah

Matthew—Jesus is the new Moses, teacher of the new law

Luke—Jesus, filled with the Holy Spirit, is Savior of all

John—Jesus is the Word of God made flesh

Differing in culture, geography, time, and emphasis, these various writers make clear that from the beginning there has been more than one christology in the Christian community. All confessing the same faith, they articulate this in a pluralism of ways. Taken together, their writings form the Christian scriptures, foundational to doing christology now since they carry the remembrance and witness of the inspired early communities.

2. Conciliar Christology (Second through Seventh Centuries)

As the church moved into the wider Hellenistic world, preaching and thinking made use of philosophical categories that were a common part of the Mediterranean culture. These categories of Greek philosophy abstracted from knowledge of the way things act or function to raise the question of what things are in themselves, formulating this in terms such as nature, subsistence, and the like. While the early biblical communities had concentrated on what God had done for them in Jesus, and consequently on who Jesus is in a functional way, these later Hellenistic communities, made up almost exclusively of Gentiles (non-Jews), began to wonder about Jesus in an ontological way. In other words, from proclaiming what he does—Jesus saves—their questions moved to the order of being: Who is he in himself that enables him to function as our Savior? From understanding that he is from God, their probing raised the question of his relation to the one and only God named Father. Were there two Gods? Unthinkable. Was Jesus a lesser god? Thinkable, but then how could he truly save? How could Jesus Christ be God and God the Father be God, and still there be only one God? In addition, questions about his relation to the human race became acute. If he is truly from God, then is he truly human? Is his body real flesh? Does he have a human soul with genuine human psychology? If not, then is the incarnation only a pretense? But if so, then is he really two persons, human and divine? If he is truly human how can he be considered at the same time truly divine and still be one person? All of these questions were phrased according to the idiom of the day, so that people of the church were involved in their development.

Debate raged over Jesus Christ's identity. One bishop went out to buy a loaf of bread and wrote later that "even the baker" wanted to discuss whether there were one or two natures in Christ!

There were two tendencies causing problems. On the one hand, some wanted to downplay any identity between God and the human being Jesus—in the end he is only a creature. He is definitely a superior creature, so said the priest Arius, but God cannot share being with anything finite or limited. To call Jesus "God" would be to dishonor God by involving the divine with limited flesh. So "God" is applied to Jesus as a courtesy title only. In 325 at the Council of Nicea, the bishops of the East decided that this approach was false. In the creed that they wrote, the Nicene creed still said and sung in the church today, Jesus is confessed as "God from God, Light from Light, true God from true God; begotten not made; one in being with the Father." If this were not true, they reasoned, we would not be saved by Jesus. For sin is so strong that no mere creature can overcome it; "only God can save."

On the other hand, some thinkers so stressed the divinity of Jesus Christ that they lost sight of his real humanity. Some examples show how far this tendency went:

> For he ate, not for the sake of the body, which was kept together by a holy energy, but in order that it might not enter into the mind of those who were with him to entertain a different opinion of him.—Clement of Alexandria

> Our Lord felt the force of suffering but without its pain; the nails pierced his flesh as an object passes through the air, painlessly.—Hilary of Poitiers

> Middle beings are formed when different properties are combined in one thing, e.g., the properties of ass and horse in a

mule, and the properties of white and black in the color gray. But no middle being contains the two extremes in full measures, but only in part. Now in Christ there is a middle-being of God and man; therefore he is neither fully man nor God alone, but a mixture of God and man.—Bishop Apollinarius

This approach was also found to be false by the Council of Constantinople in 381. The Eastern bishops reasoned that we are saved by God taking on fully whatever belongs to human nature; if something is not assumed in the incarnation, it is not redeemed. Thus Jesus' genuine and integral humanity becomes a salvific truth.

Between these two extreme tendencies, the church struggled to maintain a full appreciation of Jesus' identification both with God and with human beings. As Pope Leo I wrote, "It is as dangerous an evil to deny the truth of the human nature of Christ as it is to refuse to believe that his glory is equal to the Father." Finally, in A.D. 451 after years of debate and episodes of unseemly conduct, the Council of Chalcedon affirmed this insight of faith. In Hellenistic terms they confessed Jesus Christ to be one in being with the Father as to divinity, and one in being with us as to humanity; truly God and truly human, having a rational soul. He is one and the same Christ made known in two natures which come together in one person.

3. Medieval Christology (Eleventh through Sixteenth Centuries)

During this period no major controversies existed about Christ, although some minor ones erupted. The main change came with the introduction of a new process of reasoning and synthesizing identified with scholasticism. Within the sociological context of feudalism, Anselm of Canterbury explored why God became a human being and had to *die* to save us, for could it not have been done in a different way? He reasoned brilliantly that Jesus Christ dies in order to make satisfaction for sin, without which the order of the universe would be forever disturbed.

In the universities, a new locale for theology, scholars explained the two-natures-in-one-person schema with the help of Aristotle's newly rediscovered philosophy. Imbued with piety, some thinkers sought to honor Jesus Christ by reasoning according to the principle of perfection. This held that it was not fitting to deny to Christ's human nature any perfection which it might have had. Accordingly, they envisioned him as the perfect sailor, the perfect mathematician, even the perfect canon lawyer!

At the end of this period, the Protestant reformers called for a stop to scholastic metaphysical speculation about Christ's inner constitution, and a return to a more existential, biblically based confession of Jesus Christ who won salvation on the cross and whose grace saves us now without any merit on our part. To know Christ is to know his benefits, Luther argued, not to know refinements of dogma.

4. Post-Tridentine Christology (Sixteenth through Twentieth Centuries)

In face of the threat of the Reformation, and following this, the threat of the modern world moving toward democracy and challenging traditional authorities, the Catholic church assumed a largely defensive posture. It drew the wagons around to protect its great heritage, but by and large refused to engage new questions posed by the modern world. Along with other areas of theology, christology was organized into tract or manual format in which a thesis of doctrine was followed by certain logical deductions, the whole supported by classical arguments and each element assigned a specific theological weight. This format lent itself to memorization if not to intelligible understanding. In the United States the manual format was adapted into the question-answer pattern of the *Baltimore Catechism*, a catechetical tool that taught the official christological answer to generations of immigrant children. The dryness of this intellectual approach was supplemented by a rich devotional life including devotion to the Sacred Heart, Stations of the Cross, and other practices of a Jesus piety.

5. At the Brink of Renewal (1951)

This year saw the celebration of the Council of Chalcedon which fifteen hundred years earlier had confessed Jesus Christ to be truly God and truly a human being, two natures in one person. This anniversary clearly marks the beginning of a renewal in Catholic christology, for many studies done by scholars around the world sought to probe the original meaning of that council's affirmations, finding it richer than neo-scholastic interpretation had allowed.

Among the many commemorative essays written that year, the one by theologian Karl Rahner originally entitled "Chalcedon, End or Beginning?" has had a lasting impact. Surveying the Catholic scene, Rahner judged that christology was in a sorry and stagnant state. The use of manuals which explained Christ in deductive logic gave the impression that we knew Christ thoroughly and definitively. This prevented new insights from arising. Furthermore, this manual approach tended to ignore the wealth of scripture with its narration of the events of Jesus' life, such as his baptism, prayer to God, and abandonment on the cross. All of this was left to piety or meditation but did not inform intellectual efforts to understand and confess Jesus Christ. Christology was just repeating old neo-scholastic understanding about two natures in one person without genuine contemporary understanding. The cumulative effect of all these elements was that christology by and large ignored the genuine humanity of Jesus Christ, a matter of scriptural and dogmatic truth. As a sign that christology was moribund Rahner applied the interesting criterion of controversy. How few really living and passionate controversies there are in Catholic christology today, he bemoaned, which engage the existential concern of the faithful—can you name a single one? We had made the dogma of Chalcedon an end in itself, whereas it should always be a beginning of thought since it carries the richness of the mystery of God's presence in the midst of our suffering history.

Since 1951 significant developments both within and without the church have made the question "Who do you say that I am?" alive once again. The Second Vatican Council, while not focusing to any extent on christology, encouraged the church to dialogue with the joys and sorrows, the hopes and fears of the modern world. When we turned to do so, we found a world very different from the medieval world where dialogue, for the most part, had last occurred. Three shifts in the modern intellectual history of Europe stand out as having particular influence on Catholic theology since the council, and thereby on christology.

In the first place chronologically is what is called "the turn to the subject." Associated with the work of the German philosopher Immanual Kant, this shift places attention squarely on the human person as a free subject in the process of becoming. As a corollary, human experience becomes an important norm for human knowing, a move which brings into question the dominance of authority and tradition. Further associated with this turn is a fascination with history and historical methods, with how things came to be in time.

As this turn to the subject has intersected with christology, it has given rise to interest in the founding experiences of the faith. There is real interest now in Jesus as a genuine human subject, a real historical person with his own personal traits and life story. It has also awakened new interest in the experiences of the disciples who founded the Christian faith and to our own experiences as followers of Jesus today. The question arises: What has Jesus Christ got to do with our becoming fully human, free persons?

A second major shift involves the turn to the negativity of so much human experience. Two world wars, the Holocaust, the Gulag, colonialism, the greed and narcissism of capitalism, torture as an instrument of state policy, political oppression, apartheid, the ecological crisis, the threat of nuclear disaster—all of these evils and more have turned thoughtful attention to the suffering of people in history and to those who are history's victims. A new sensitivity both to the irrational and to human pathology, individual and social, now affects thinking.

In christology the impact of this turn has been felt in the recovery of the relevance of Jesus' ministry with his preaching of the reign of God, a symbol with social and political implications. The interpretation of the cross grapples with the significance of why Jesus did not die a natural death but was executed. The value of the demonic and of apocalyptic as symbolic elements of thought has come to light. The good news that God comes to save us takes on new and specific power. An entire change in christological method is involved as the question is raised: How does praxis, or doing the truth in love, or action on behalf of justice, become a path of knowledge about Jesus Christ?

A third major shift is a turn to the whole globe as one small and interconnected world. From telecommunications to instruments of mass death, all peoples and all living things are affected by the actions of one another. At this point we realize how interdependent we are while not yet having structures to support and develop this in a positive direction. While some prize dominance, others search for a new transcultural humanity in which ethnic particularity is prized while the human race is valued as one. In this context, the religions are newly encountering one another and becoming newly aware of one another's wisdom, especially in face of the death-dealing powers of this world.

→ In christology, this shift of consciousness is giving rise to a whole new slate of questions. What does the uniqueness of Jesus Christ as Savior of the world mean in the encounter with the world religions? Is it possible to believe that God has acted decisively in Jesus Christ to save the whole world, and simultaneously to believe that Jews, Moslems, Hindus, Buddhists, and persons of other religious persuasions are warranted in remaining who they are, pursuing the paths of salvation on which they find themselves? Who do we say that Christ is in view of the fact that millions of people do not follow any religious path at all, and yet we hope they are saved by the same mercy of God revealed in Jesus Christ?

In the chapters that follow we will be exploring the response which theology is making to these great shifts in human experience and consciousness. The intersection of contemporary experience with the heritage of faith is not without difficulty. The Catholic community now has more than enough living and passionate controversies in christology which engage the concern of the faithful. Rahner today would be a happy man! For these debates over the interpretation of Jesus Christ are signs of a living tradition in a church which has moved with its faith out of a self-imposed ghetto into genuine dialogue with contemporary problems. Since the middle of the twentieth century, the issues in christology have emerged more or less sequentially, like waves breaking on a beach. We trace these rising developments in christology not out of intellectual interest alone, although it makes a fascinating story. But even more we ponder these things because, guided by scripture and tradition which carry the faith of our ancestors, we are responsible for answering the great christological question in our own time and place: "But who do you say that I am?"

Readings

Out of the immense literature on Jesus Christ the following works are offered as a guide to readers who may wish to pursue a particular point further. One of the most readable overviews of the Catholic theological tradition about Jesus Christ is Gerard Sloyan, *The Jesus Tradition: Images of Jesus in the West* (Mystic, CN: Twenty-Third Pubns., 1986); George Tavard, *Images of Christ: An Enquiry into Christology* (Lanham, MD: University Press of America, 1982), covers the same ground in a more technical way. In a broader context Jaroslav Pelikan, *Jesus Through the Centuries: His Place in the History of Culture* (New Haven, CN: Yale University Press, 1985), presents a fascinating, readable survey of eighteen images of Jesus in relation to shifting cultural mores.

The dynamism of biblical christology's development of names for Jesus is captured by James Dunn, *Christology in the Making: A New Testament Inquiry into the Origins of the Doctrine of the Incarnation* (Philadelphia: Westminster, 1980). The diversity of New Testament christologies is presented in clear prose by Reginald Fuller and Pheme Perkins, *Who Is This Christ? Gospel Christology and Contemporary Faith* (Philadelphia: Fortress, 1983). Jerome Neyrey, *Christ Is Community: The Christologies of the New Testament* (Wilmington, DL: Glazier, 1985), explores this diversity from the viewpoint of the social sciences which understands texts from the types of communities that produced them.

The disputes surrounding the early church councils and their decisions in the realm of christology are set out by J.N.D. Kelly, *Early Christian Doctrines* (New York: Harper & Row, 1978), and by Jaroslav Pelikan, *The Emergence of the Catholic Tradition* (Chicago: University of Chicago Press, 1971). Richard Norris, *The Christological Controversy* (Philadelphia: Fortress, 1980), has edited pertinent original texts. Very useful is Frances Young, *From*

Nicea to Chalcedon: A Guide to the Literature and Its Background (Philadelphia: Fortress, 1984).

One of the most accessible examples of scholastic reasoning in christology remains Anselm's *Cur Deus Homo?* (in English, *Why God Became Man* [Albany, NY: Magi Books, 1969]), structured as a dialogue between the wise Anselm and his inquiring student Boso. Zachary Hayes, *The Hidden Center: Spirituality and Speculative Christology in St. Bonaventure* (New York: Paulist, 1981), captures the flavor of this unique blend in another outstanding medieval scholastic. Given the split between the universities and the people, much christology went forward in devotion. *Jesus in Christian Devotion and Contemplation,* trans. Paul Oligny (St. Meinrad, IN: Abbey Press, 1974), pays particular attention to medieval and late medieval approaches. See also the essays by John Meyendorff, "Christ as Savior in the East," 231–52, and Bernard McGinn, "Christ as Savior in the West," 253–59, in *Christian Spirituality: Origins to the Twelfth Century,* Bernard McGinn et al., eds. (New York: Crossroad, 1985); and Ewert Cousins, "The Humanity and the Passion of Christ," 375–91, in *Christian Spirituality: High Middle Ages and Reformation,* Jill Raitt, ed. (New York: Crossroad, 1987).

Marc Lienhard, *Luther, Witness to Jesus Christ* (Minneapolis: Augsburg, 1982), traces the themes and stages of development in the reformer's christology. An excellent example of Catholic christology before Vatican II is Karl Adam, *The Christ of Faith: The Christology of the Church* (New York: Pantheon Books, 1957); his own early attempt to encourage appreciation of the humanity of Christ is *Christ Our Brother* (New York: Macmillan, 1931), which bears the marks of having been written before the biblical renewal. The pivotal essay in which Karl Rahner analyzes difficulties in the state of christology and suggests a way forward has as its English title "Current Problems in Christology," *Theological Investigations* 1 (Baltimore: Helicon, 1961), 149–200. Another analysis of the same situation is Yves Congar, *Christ, Our Lady and the Church* (London: Longmans, Green, 1957).

One of the best descriptions of modern influences on christology and the discussion of Jesus Christ since the council is William M. Thompson, *The Jesus Debate: A Survey and Synthesis* (New York:

Paulist, 1985), which also makes its own constructive suggestions toward a christology of love, justice, and peace. Of interest both for what it reveals and does not reveal is the poll by George Gallup, *Who Do Americans Say That I Am?* (Philadelphia: Westminster, 1986).

2

The Humanity of Jesus

It is interesting to note that in the mid-twentieth century while Protestant communions were deeply embroiled in controversy over the interpretation of scripture and consequently over how to understand the historical Jesus, Catholic christology which had concentrated for centuries on dogma began its revival in this doctrinal field. The first wave of renewal in Catholic christology clearly rose in the 1950's and early 1960's during the celebration of the Council of Chalcedon, fifteen hundred years old in 1951. Theologians marked the occasion by doing what they do best, writing studies. Their deep look at that council's doctrine about Christ led to a new appreciation of what it was affirming and an analysis of the shortcomings in the way people had come to understand it. Karl Rahner, whose influential essay has already been mentioned, was joined in this endeavor by European theologians such as Hans Urs von Balthasar, Piet Schoonenberg, Bernhard Welte, and Bernard Lonergan, a Canadian teaching in Rome.

Chalcedon had confessed that the identity of Jesus Christ was to be understood as comprised of two natures, a human nature and a divine nature, which came together in the unity of one person. The problem that these theologians identified did not lie with that confession in itself. Rather, the problem was found to exist with the way this dogma had come to be

19

taught and understood. For theology had forgotten the mystery of salvation which was being safeguarded in the language of this doctrine, and had made its concepts too clear and its ideas too distinct.

On the one hand, there was the issue of the two natures in Jesus Christ. The fact that these categories point to a mysterious reality was overlooked, especially in the manuals. Instead, the two natures had come to be understood as two varieties of the same basic thing, two species of one genus, something like apples and oranges are two kinds of the one category fruit. The point that divine nature is holy mystery, in a class by itself and in no way comparable to human or any other kind of nature, had simply slipped from view. Consequently, when people, including theologians, said that Jesus had two natures, they implicitly thought of each of these natures as comprising one-half the total picture. Jesus became so to speak, 50/50, partly divine and partly human, or totally divine and partly human, but not truly divine and truly human, 100/100 as Chalcedon had confessed.

On the other hand, there was the problem of understanding the language of one "person." What is a person? The meaning of this word today in a post-Freudian era is very different from what it was in fifth-century thought. The word today usually connotes a psychological entity, an individual center of consciousness and freedom, constituted in relation to other persons in a community. However, the Greek word *hypostasis* originally used in the doctrine is not a psychological but a philosophical term that connoted something ontological, in the order of being. It meant subsistence, or the metaphysical root of a thing, or the firm ground from out of which an existing individual stands forth and exists. There is no simple English word which would translate its meaning exactly. Thus there has been a semantic drift with the meaning of the word "person"; it has slipped out from under the church's dogmatic meaning. To modern ears a psychological twist is given to the confession that Jesus Christ is the Second "Person" of the Blessed Trinity, so that little or no room exists for his real human psychology to function.

The first wave of renewal in christology grappled with the ancient dogma to unlock once again its original faith affirmations: that in dealing with Jesus we are dealing with the one God who alone is God, who is one of us, and who is both of these in unbreakable unity—and all of this for the sake of our salvation. Given the basic tendency in the Catholic approach of the time to think of Jesus as more divine than human, this effort had the result of recovering the genuine humanity of Jesus as dogmatically defined. Let us take each of the doctrinal terms: human nature, divine nature, one person. We will trace the pattern of thought about the meaning of these terms which Catholic theologians of the 1950's developed. Rather than using classical scholastic philosophy which would define a person as an individual substance of a rational nature, these theologians applied existential philosophy developing in Europe at the time. Their approach is still heavily philosophical, but in a newer mode. It is usually called transcendental theology, for they seek to make dogma meaningful by connecting it with anthropology, with human existence analyzed by transcendental methods.

Human Nature

What is human nature? Let us try to get at this by means of some simple experiences. A person asks a question. This is a universally human thing to do—young children, old people, persons of every race and tongue, people of all ages. Asking a question is a characteristic of human beings, as unique to us as a species as is laughing. What does asking a question reveal about ourselves?

It shows first of all that we do not know some thing and yet want to know it: we have a desire for this truth, whatever the

answer will be. It also means in some significant way that we
do have a hunch that something is there to be known, or we
could not even ask the question to begin with. Asking a
question reveals that we are in touch with a known unknown.
When we receive an answer to our question, do we stop
asking questions? No. Curiosity drives us on, and every answer can well be the foundation for the next question. We ask
not just about practical matters such as how things work and
why the sky is blue, but also about very deep issues such as
what is the meaning of our life and why there is so much
suffering in the world. How many questions can we ask in a
lifetime? It is without number. No one answer will ultimately
satisfy us.

The human spirit is revealed by this analysis as having an
infinite thirst for truth and an infinite capacity for truth, an
infinite dynamism toward truth. We can keep on asking questions and keep on receiving answers, but it does not shut us
down; rather, it keeps awakening us further. One of the worst
sins persons can commit is to stop asking questions, because
then they are prematurely dead inside; they have quenched the
spirit. This questioning of our dynamic spirit reveals that we
are thirsty for the truth and that we have a capacity for it that
does not ever get filled up. Now at this point we raise the
question: Are human beings ever fulfilled? Does this quest of
ours for truth ever reach a resting point? Obviously not in this
world. The only reality that will quench this quest of ours is
God's own being which is infinite truth, Truth itself.

Existentialist philosophers would agree with Catholic theologians that human beings are open to the infinite and are
dynamically questing for the infinite; but they would disagree
about whether or not there is ever a fulfillment. For example
John Paul Sartre, the atheist philosopher, argued that there is
no fulfillment ever to be had. Life is a joke, it is absurd: while
we are structured toward the infinite, we are destined to

eternal frustration. Now in faith the answer would come back—no. We have an infinite thirst for truth and we are going to be satisfied only by infinite truth. However, there *is* infinite truth, and we name that God.

What this kind of analysis reveals is that human beings are dynamically moving toward the infinite and will only be satisfied by the infinite. The same kind of analysis can be made with experiences of loving. When we love someone, and are loved, it reveals a dynamism of our spirit which is boundless. Interpersonal love does not shut down our capacity for loving but rather opens it up even further. The classic example here is that of a man and a woman who love each other. Out of that love comes a new being, a child, whom they also love. The circle of love keeps growing wider. Once again the human spirit's quest for love, and capacity for love, seem to be infinite. And again the question: Is this human thirst for love ever satisfied in this life? No. Ultimately only infinite love can satisfy this thirst of ours. We call infinite Love God. So once again thinking of people's love experiences, we arrive at the same realization—that human beings are dynamically structured toward the infinite.

A third experience to trace is the experience of hoping against hope. In situations of desperate need, human beings nevertheless do not necessarily despair. We can always hope against the present for a better future. There is a capacity in us to imagine a better future and to hope against hope for it. A great deal of prison literature shows this capacity of the human spirit. Survivors of Nazi death camps, of South African detention cells, of Latin American political prisons bear witness that even when people are totally bound in, deprived of elemental necessities and treated in violent and degrading ways, the human spirit can still yearn for life beyond the present moment. This shows itself in the human capacity to imagine a different situation and to hope for it to become actual. This imaginative ability to hope against hope reveals that we have an infinite capacity for life, which ultimately can be filled only by the source of life, God, Life itself.

This analysis of human nature ends with a rather different idea of ourselves from the scholastic definition of human beings as rational animals. We are that. But in addition we are so made that we are dynamically structured toward the infinite and will only be satisfied by the infinite God. We are not a closed-off, limited reality, but open out into depth that goes all the way down to the infinite itself. There is an architectural image that symbolizes this very well. In Rome the Pantheon is an old pagan temple that has been made into a Christian church. It is round, and the roof is a great dome with a circle cut out at the top. The sun streams in, as does the rain. The church is pretty dim most of the time so that when you walk in the door you are in a gloomy enclosure, but pouring down from up above is this bright light. Your whole spirit swoops up into the light and out to the sky. That building is an image of human nature understood through transcendental analysis. We are not capped off; we are open at the top, you might say; we go off into the infinite by the very way that we are made. Augustine knew this and in a famous sentence expressed it well: "You have made us for yourself, O God, and our hearts are restless until they rest in Thee." Our restless hearts will rest only in God. Existentialist analysis is showing us that from very human activities such as asking questions, loving someone, or hoping against hope, it becomes clear that we are made for God. Christians would say that it is no accident that we are made this way. God graciously made us this way precisely in order to be able to be our fulfillment.

What is human nature? It is a finite reality with a capacity for the infinite, a thirst for the infinite. In its last issue of 1982, *Time* magazine featured the computer as "Man of the Year" and included in that issue an essay about peoples' fear that computers might take over. The author, Roger Rosenblatt, wrote:

> What if the human mind with all of its complexities could in fact be replicated in steel and plastic, and all human confusions find their way onto a software program—would the battle be lost? Hardly. . . . Even if it were possible to reduce people to box size and have them sit down before themselves in all their powers, they would still want more. Whatever its source there is a desire in us that out-desires desire; otherwise computers themselves would not have come into being. As fast as the mind travels, it somehow manages to travel faster than itself, and people always know or sense that they still do not know. No machine does that. A computer can achieve what it does not know (not knowing that 2 plus 2 equals 4, it can find out). But it cannot yearn for the answer or even dimly suspect its existence. If people knew where such suspicion and yearnings came from, they might be able to lock them in silicon. But they do not know where they come from; they merely know that they are. In the end the difference between us and any machine we create is that a machine is an answer, and we are a question.

This writer echoes in a different context the insight of mid-century Catholic theologians. Human nature as a definable concept cannot be totally grasped. Our own mystery goes deeper than that. We are a question more than we are an answer. The first step in the 1950's renewal of christology was recovering this deep mystery of what it means to be human, both for ourselves and for Jesus.

Divine Nature

If we are a mystery, how much more is God a mystery? God's own being (divine nature) is utterly incomprehensible to us. We cannot grasp God in a single concept, or a word, or an image, or a name, or definition. Whoever God is keeps slipping away from our naming into the deep mystery of the divinity. If that were not true, then God would not be God. This is a very classic doctrine. Recall the story of St. Augustine walking on the beach, trying to figure out the mystery of the Trinity. As he watched a little child with a pail trying to put the sea into a hole he had dug in the sand, Augustine said, "You cannot do that." To this the child (actually an angel) replied, "Neither can you fit the mystery of the Trinity into your finite mind." Whether or not this actually happened, it is an excellent story about our fundamental situation before God. Augustine was later to write that, "If you have understood, then what you have understood is not God." By the nature of things we are finite, we are creatures, talking here of the infinite God who has created us. So we cannot understand God.

Even though God is a profound mystery, we go on boldly in the Christian faith to proclaim that God is the profound mystery of love. In fact the New Testament sums God up in one word: "God is love" (1 Jn 4:8). Simone Weil, the religious writer, uses a marvelous image to illustrate this when she says "God is love the way an emerald is green—He is 'I love.'" An emerald would not be an emerald without being green and God would not be God without being love, if you believe the scriptural revelation that God is love. Love is able to give itself away, love is able to pour itself out, love seeks union with the other. This is the kind of God we are talking about when we say "divine nature."

Here the problem with the word "person" comes into theology, in the doctrine of the Trinity which talks about one God in three divine persons. Most people today hear that word "person" in a contemporary sense, a psychological sense, as a center of consciousness and freedom related to other persons. This leads to the problem that in talking about the three persons in God, many Catholic people are really tritheists and think of three "people" in God: Father, a Son, and an amorphous Holy Spirit (we never quite get the Spirit personalized). Again, that is not the original meaning of the word in the doctrine of the Trinity. *Hypostasis* does not mean a person in a contemporary sense. What does it mean that God is a person? Or three persons? Whatever it means, it does not mean that God is like three individual people somehow pasted together so that in the end we are really dealing with three gods. Karl Rahner suggested that theology drop the word "person" and speak of *hypostasis* in a more original sense of distinct manner of subsistence or self-subsistence. God's own self has three different ways of being, or exists in three distinct manners of subsistence. As Rahner spells it out, God is God first of all in the divine self—the unoriginate and source of all; when we think of God that way we call God Father. Then God is God again in a way that is always self-expressing, always self-uttering, always going out; when we think of God that way we call God the Word or the Son. And God is God a third time as the power of unifying love, always bringing the divine self-expression back into the primordial unity; when we talk about God as love we call God the Holy Spirit. There is one God in three distinct ways of self-being. Some theologians such as Walter Kasper dispute Rahner's dismissal of the word "person." But the debate has helped us realize that our language about God cannot be pushed to the extreme in a literal way, a realization that is also accomplished by the doctrine of analogy in Catholic theology. The doctrine of the Trinity safeguards the understanding of divine nature as a mystery of self-communicating love.

One Person

We have seen human nature as a deep mystery questing for the infinite. We have seen divine nature as a deep mystery of self-giving love. The christological question arises when we inquire after what happens when these two enter into union in the incarnation. More often than not, in the popular mind although not in doctrine, divine nature has been thought to overshadow human nature, to diminish it, or even to swallow it up. It has always been a scandal that this one person can be truly God and really human at the same time. There has been heresy after heresy in the history of the church which has denied the genuine humanity of God in the incarnation: there was no real human body, nor real soul, nor real human will, nor real human nature. It is as though God and humanity are somehow opposed to each other, or in competition with each other, so that a choice has to be made for one or the other.

As Karl Rahner has written so extensively, this intuition has functioned widely in spirituality and asceticism, giving rise to the idea that in order to honor God and grow in holiness we must put ourselves down, be diminished, somehow get ourselves out of the way. There is a truth in this ascetic approach not to be lost sight of, namely, the fact that we are sinners. There is an egocentricism in us that needs to be called constantly to conversion. Left to our own devices, there is indeed competition between our sinful ways and what God is calling us to be.

At the same time, given the way God has created and redeemed us, we are not in competition with God but rather made for God. From our side, since we are structured toward the infinite with a capacity for truth, love, and life that knows no bounds, then the nearer we get to Truth, Love, Life—or God—the more fulfilled we are going to be. As for God, who creates and redeems out of love, God is glorified not by the diminishment but by the enhancement and growth of the beloved creature. Thus, the more human we become, the more God is pleased. As the second-century bishop Irenaeus exclaimed, "The glory of God is the human being fully alive!"

The underlying truth here can be seen best by the analogy

of human love. Parents' love for their child does not diminish the child's personhood but enables the child to grow into a mature human being. Good married love transforms the married partners into being fully themselves as individuals the more united they become in their own love. The love of friendship has a similar effect, enabling friends to flourish as human beings. Could anything less be true of God who is Love? God's drawing near is creative of mature and full humanity. One could appeal here to the saints; the most popular saints, at any rate, have a very winning humanity about them (Francis of Assisi, for example). Again, what usually attracts young people to a life of deeply committed faith or even to a religious vocation is more often than not the humanity of someone who is already in that life. The goodness that is shown, the humor, the personal maturity, is very attractive, and the young person rightly senses this as a sign of holiness, of union with God as its source.

Experience shows that the closer we become to God, then the more fully our own true selves we become, rather than less ourselves. As Karl Rahner challenges us to think, "Nearness to God and genuine human autonomy grow in direct and not inverse proportion." The more fully human one becomes, the more God is taking hold. What, then, of Jesus?

In the case of Jesus of Nazareth we are dealing with someone who was more profoundly united to God than any one of us. We even talk about hypostatic union, a union at the metaphysical level of the person. If his humanity is united with God in this most profound way, what are we to say about him as a human being? That he is genuinely human, and in fact more human, more free, more alive, more his own person than any of us, because his union with God is more profound. Rather than seeing the humanity and divinity as opposites, if one thinks of humanity flourishing the nearer one is to God, then in Jesus' case the logic applies that since he of all our race is the most profoundly united with God, then in fact he is the most fully human and free. Rather than the confession of his divinity diminishing his humanity in our imagination, it should in fact release him to be a fully free human being. Because of the incarnation, he does not become less human but rather the most fully human of us all. One can go to the scriptures and see sign after sign of this: he is like us in all things, tempted in every way that we are, yet without sin (Heb 4:15–5:3).

As a genuinely human being, Jesus Christ is God with us. This is made thinkable with the help of the biblical concept of *kenosis,* or self-emptying. At the moment of the incarnation, God who is love eternally self-expressing within the divine being as the eternal Word, self-expresses outwardly into the history of this earth. God's own inner Word is spoken into the medium of human flesh, bringing Jesus into existence. God who is always self-expressing within the divine nature now self-expresses outside the divine nature, in time, in human nature, in another medium (you might say), and the one who comes into existence is Jesus of Nazareth, the Word made flesh. In addition to speaking of God's "assuming" human nature, as classical theology does, we can think of this as a moment of *kenosis* or God's "self-emptying" of the glory of divine nature. As Paul wrote of Jesus, "although he was by nature God, he did not consider being equal to God something to be clung to, but emptied himself, taking the nature of a servant" (Phil 2:6–7). Jesus Christ comes into existence as God's own self-expression in time, himself genuinely human, with the divine glory veiled. If we do not think of God literally as three different people but rather as the triune mystery of self-giving love, then it becomes possible to see Jesus existing as the Word of God in time who, in his humanness, embodies the self-emptying of the God of love.

At the end of this thinking anew about the dogma of Chalcedon, each of its words comes to mean something related to our lives. Human nature is a deep questing mystery, thirsting for the infinite. Divine nature is the incomprehensible mystery of holy Love seeking to give Godself away. The two come together in the incarnation in a personal unity which enables the human nature of Jesus to flourish. In this way of reading the dogma we do not say, "Jesus is God, and in addition human as well." Rather, we start at the other end and say, "As this human being, Jesus is the Son of God. Precisely as this human being he is God in time. He is fully human, fully free, fully personal, and as such he is God who has self-emptied into our history." At the end of this progression of thought, what is restored to our consciousness is a way of envisioning Jesus to be genuinely human at the same time that the confession of his genuine divinity does not slip from view.

Conclusion

The significance of this approach has continued to affect the church since this work was done in the 1950's and early 1960's. The fact that Jesus is genuinely human came as a bit of a surprise to Catholics at first. What should have been part of our consciousness all along, and was officially part of doctrine, has taken time to be fully realized. Vatican II's *The Church in the Modern World (Gaudium et Spes, 22)* ringingly affirmed this recovery of Jesus Christ's humanity, stating in one beautiful passage:

> Human nature as he assumed it was not annulled. . . . He worked with human hands, he thought with a human mind, he acted by human choice, and loved with a human heart. Born of the Virgin Mary, he has truly been made one of us, like us in all things except sin.

This paragraph has been quoted by every Pope since the council in very significant ways. For example, in his first encyclical, John Paul II uses the text to speak of the dignity of human beings, an enormous dignity due not only to the fact that we have been created by God, but also thanks to the way that we are united to the Redeemer, whose own humanity sheds light on ours *(Redemptor Hominis, 8)*.

The consciousness of Jesus' humanity is flowing into our conversation again in the church and is having ramifications in many areas. What does this mean in terms of spirituality? It has led to revaluation of the humanness of all of us in a very positive direction. Formation programs in religious communities, preaching, spiritual direction, and so on, communicate a sense that each of us as human is a gift of God, filled with potency for God; a sense that human nature itself is moving in the direction of God. There is a different emphasis in spirituality growing out of this, a different kind of asceticism, a much more positive view of our humanness. Again, in terms of ethics, the direction of thinking has been this: If God has become one of us and Jesus Christ as a fully human being is confessed as God, then the humanity of every single human being in some implicit way (because we are all one race) is also united with God and has its own very special dignity. The logic is clear: If God has become one of us, then that means something for the whole human race. Human nature itself is gifted with God's identification with us in our own nature. Again, both the council and John Paul II have insisted, "Human nature, by the very fact that it was assumed, not absorbed, in him has been raised in us also to a dignity beyond compare" *(Gaudium et Spes 22; Redemptor Hominis 8)*. This leads to a very strong sense in the church of the dignity of every human being precisely as human, and to a very strong social teaching with regard to human rights. The church's social teaching is not based only on simple humanism, but on a deep christological motif: God has so identified with our humanity that each of us as human beings has been lifted to a dignity beyond compare. Thus, whatever disfigures or damages a human being is an insult to God's own self. In a more poetic way, Karl Rahner has envisioned that because of the Word of God in our midst, it can now be seen that each of us is a little word of God. The one Word of God uttered in our midst reveals to us our own beauty, for we are each a little word and together we will spell out something great. Again, he describes each of us as a letter of the alphabet; when we are all assembled we will spell out a great word to the glory of God: "Human nature is the grammar of God's self-utterance." Our human nature is so made that God can speak in and through us. All of this flows out of the incarnation, which is real and not a pretense on God's part. That God actually became one of us leads us to value all human beings as gifted with a tremendous dignity precisely as human.

Karl Rahner, in his groundbreaking essay in 1951, questioned whether Chalcedon should be an end or a beginning-ever-anew for Christian reflection. He argued that we need to start our thinking from it, rather than sit with it as an accomplishment. A whole generation of Catholic scholars joined him in the search for its meaning. The result is the recovery of the full humanity of Jesus Christ as dogma, and a new appreciation of the incomparable dignity of every human being.

Readings

The anthropological starting point for christology is carefully and beautifully set out in Karl Rahner, *Foundations of Christian Faith* (New York: Seabury, 1978), which, while a tough read, rewards slow scrutiny. This may be illuminated by Leo O'Donovan, ed., *A World of Grace* (New York: Seabury, 1980), which describes both the context and broad themes of Rahner's theology in a readable way. While condensed in chapter 6 of *Foundations*, two essays in their whole form show the range and depth of Rahner's rethinking: "On the Theology of the Incarnation," *Theological Investigations* 4 (New York: Seabury, 1974), 105–20; and "Christology Within an Evolutionary View of the World," *Theological Investiga-*

tions 5 (Baltimore: Helicon, 1966), 157–92. Another influential work which sets Jesus' humanity within the context of broad theological themes is Piet Schoonenberg, *The Christ: A Study of the God-Man Relationship in the Whole of Creation and in Jesus Christ* (New York: Herder & Herder, 1971).

3

Jesus' Self-Knowledge

One particular subquestion surfaced strongly in the 1950's as part of the wider issue of the true humanity of Jesus. This is the question of his own knowledge of things and particularly of himself. A naive approach can quickly lead into a double bind. If Jesus knew he was the Word of God, then how could he be genuinely human? Think of what kind of human life you would live knowing you were God! It would remove you from the zone of limits within which human life is lived. But if he did not know his own identity, then he must not be God, for God knows everything. It became immediately obvious to Catholic scholars that the project of recovering an understanding of Jesus' genuine humanity would succeed or fail, especially in the minds of Catholic people, depending on how the question of Jesus' self-knowledge was answered.

Background

It is important to note that this is a question that has never been defined by the church in any official way, so there is a lot of room here for speculation. The scriptures show Jesus as obviously knowing a great deal. He has a special sense of himself, of his mission, of his God whom he calls *Abba,* and of other people. He is no dope (so to speak) but a very astute and sensitive person; some people even think he can read their minds. At the same time the scriptures point out rather un-selfconsciously that Jesus also had limited knowledge in certain ways. One key verse is Mark 13:32 where Jesus is depicted as saying, "As to that day or hour, no one knows; not the angels in heaven; not even the Son, but only the Father." He is basically saying that like anybody else he does not know the day of the end of the world. There are a number of other similar sayings where Jesus seems to have normal limited human knowledge.

In the patristic period many debates centered around this issue. Following the witness of the scripture several ecumenical councils defined in very clear terms that Jesus had a genuine human soul and a genuine human psychology with a mind and will like everyone else. His was a true human nature with a rational soul. A spokesman for the opposite position was Appollinarius, a bishop who was a great champion of the divinity of Christ. He could not fathom that Jesus' knowledge and freedom might be limited. Instead, he designed the idea that while Jesus Christ had a real human body, he had no human soul. Instead, God the Word substituted for his human soul. Consequently, Jesus looked like a human being externally, but on the inside his psychology was divine. In his 1951 analysis Karl Rahner judged that the ghost of Appollinarius still haunts the Church; many people still think that Jesus Christ does not have a truly human psychology, but that his body houses the mind of God.

In the Middle Ages, the idea that Jesus has a genuine human nature was firmly in place but theology, under pressure of culture, began to gift his human nature with all kinds of knowledge above and beyond ordinary human knowledge. Thomas Aquinas was typical of his era in holding that Jesus Christ had three kinds of special human knowledge: beatific vision, infused knowledge, and experimental knowledge.

1. Even while on earth, he had the knowledge of God given in the beatific vision, the knowledge that comes from seeing

God face to face. This opinion was grounded in the argument
of fittingness: Jesus is the Son of God, greater in dignity than
anyone else. Would it be fitting that some people who have
died see God face to face whereas the Son of God on earth
does not? A sense of propriety and right order led theologians
to argue that Jesus had the beatific vision of God from the
moment of his conception. Aquinas for one had trouble rec-
onciling this with the agony on the cross, especially the cry of
Jesus: "My God, my God, why have you abandoned me?"
(Mk 15:34). How could Jesus be blissfully seeing God face to
face, as those in heaven do, and still be experiencing this
abandonment? The solution proposed was that in the upper
reaches of his soul he was enjoying the bliss of heaven, but in
his lower soul, the sensate soul, he was experiencing abandonment by God. Owing to modern psychology, this medieval
solution does not really work for us. Nevertheless this is what
Catholic theology had to deal with in the 1950's, for it had
been common teaching for seven hundred years.

2. While on earth Jesus Christ also had infused knowledge
of all things. This is the kind of knowledge derived from ideas
put directly into the mind by God. The angels have this kind
of knowledge since they do not have bodies and cannot glean
information from their senses. Whatever the angels know they
know it directly from God, through ideas put right into their
minds. Would it be fitting that the angels of God know things
past, present, and future through infused knowledge, whereas
the Son of God on earth does not? No. Thus it was logically
argued that Jesus knew everything past, present, and to come
while he was on earth by virtue of these infused ideas.

3. Jesus had experimental knowledge or acquired knowledge, the kind of knowledge we get by trial and error. We have
to learn, for example, how to walk, how to talk, how to eat,
etc. Some, including Aquinas, thought that Jesus never had to
learn from anyone but always taught these things to himself;
again, it would not be fitting that anyone should teach the Son

of God, given his great dignity. Furthermore, in this area of
acquired knowledge the Middle Ages speculated that Jesus
knew everything there was to know and knew it perfectly.
Obviously this idea was influenced by the growth of sciences
and arts at the medieval universities. It did not seem fitting
that some people would have knowledge of such things that
Jesus himself would not have had.

In Christian teaching and preaching, Jesus was pictured as
knowing everything—knowing God face to face; knowing
everything past, present, and to come; knowing all human
skills. Granted, he knew all of this as a human being, but
certainly as a human being gifted far beyond the rest of us
mere mortals. The results showed in the imagination of faith
where, in Rahner's analysis, Jesus Christ appears more
mythological than as a real human being. The challenge
became how to envision Jesus' human knowledge as truly
human in a credible way, without in any way compromising
the confession of his divinity. In the 1950's and 1960's there
were bitter fights on this question, and the matter is still not
totally resolved. One theological proposal, however, that of
Karl Rahner, has had a fair measure of acceptance and is
coherent with the developing christology of the last decades. I
do not think it is the last word! But it offers a way forward out
of the double bind. We will take a look at it in two steps,
asking first of all about our self-knowledge and then applying
this to Jesus, who is like us in all things except sin.

Human Consciousness

Human consciousness is a multilayered reality. We speak
today of the conscious, the preconscious, subconscious, the
unconscious levels of the mind. They are each some form of
"conscious," but bring with them different ways of knowing.
We can know something in our unconscious mind but not be
able to express it in clear words; it is known at another level.

Sometimes an incident may bring this very clearly into focus. We may have a friend or live with someone in community or in the family who is acting disturbed. It registers in our mind at a subconscious level and we do not think about it, until someday there is an explosion and this person blows up. Then we say yes, I knew there was something wrong. We knew it on one level but not explicitly in a conscious way. It is not totally accurate, then, to say we either know something or we do not. There is a way both to know *and* not to know what is outside of ourselves, both at the same time.

With regard to knowing ourselves, the dynamic is the same. We both know and do not know ourselves at the same time, in different modes or at different levels of consciousness. At least two different forms of self-knowledge can be distinguished. Subjectively, we know ourselves from within intuitively as the person we are. This is not knowledge in the form of clear ideas, but a pre-thematic self-awareness. It is a kind of presence to ourselves as a subject that accompanies and undergirds all our particular actions and thoughts. It is reflected in the consciousness we have of ourselves when we wake up in the morning: each of us comes into the new day with a unique sense of ourself as the person we are. We do not announce it; rather, it is a presence to ourselves, a grasp of ourselves, a plain and simple self-awareness that informs all of our actions. Technically this is called the transcendental pole of self-awareness.

Secondly, in a more ordinary, objective sense of knowledge, we can express facts about ourselves in clear, precise terms: our name, age, occupation, preferences, etc. This is an objective knowledge in which we know ourselves in words and concepts and can explain ourselves to others. The different experiences of life help us to know ourselves more precisely in this way, to get ourselves into words in a more concrete way. This thematic form of self-knowledge is technically called the categorical pole of self-understanding.

Throughout our lives various historical experiences provide the occasion for us to translate our intuitive self-awareness at the transcendental pole into words and concepts at the categorical pole. We are always the same person; our identity remains the same although we may develop mightily. But success, failures, those who love us or hate us, what we choose to do or fail to do, all help us to spell ourselves out in a more concrete way as life goes on. We move the intuitive knowledge we have of ourselves up front into objective knowledge. While many people go through life without doing much of this, it is something that everyone does to some extent. And it is a lifelong process. We grow in objective knowledge of ourselves, knowing more about who we are at age forty than age twenty, and so on. As long as we are drawing breath, there is still a possibility of further objective knowledge as new experiences and our reactions to them reveal us anew to ourselves. The dynamic as we know it ends only at death (and we do not speculate here about what happens next!).

One final point in the anthropological sphere before moving into christology directly. When in medieval times Jesus Christ was gifted with extraordinarily great powers of human knowledge, theologians were working under the influence of the Greek cultural ideal which equated knowledge with perfection. To be perfect was to know, while ignorance was a shadow on perfection. Since Jesus was to be depicted as perfect as possible, he necessarily had to know all things. Today we are dealing with a different anthropology and a different cultural ideal. For human beings today the ideal of perfection is not knowledge but *freedom*: for the twentieth-century person, the ideal human person is someone who is free in a very deep way rather than somebody who knows everything. It is vitally important to protect the freedom of Jesus and, interestingly, here is where ignorance begins to play a positive role. In genuine, free human decisions, the future is veiled from us in some significant way, so that we sum ourselves up and hand ourselves over in real commitment without full realization of what the outcome will be. This does not mean that we do not look at the options, weigh the pros and cons, discern, and so on. But under the conditions of history and time, for real freedom to operate we must take a risk. This is essential to our freedom. We must be willing to make decisions with darkness facing us as to what the full outcome will be. This becomes obvious in one form of the marriage ceremony, where partners take each other for better or worse, in riches or poverty, sickness or health. In other words, written right into the ceremony is the uncertainty of the future. Any vocational choice is the same, e.g., to religious life, to priesthood, to deep commitment in the face of some difficulty, whether to take this or that political action. We do not have the assurance of where it will lead but we hand ourselves over into the future, trusting that ultimately it will work out the right way. But if we human beings had full and clear foreknowledge of the future, then the condition for freedom to operate would be taken away. We would no longer be risking, no longer be handing ourselves forward in the darkness, because we would know. Human freedom as we know it would be at an end.

Jesus' Consciousness

Taking these insights—that our knowledge of ourselves has a bipolar structure, and that freedom is protected by nescience of the future—we turn to Jesus. Having a human nature like ours, his self-consciousness is structured in this bipolar way. At the subjective level of his own person he has a sense of himself, a pre-thematic consciousness of who he is. Now, who is he? He is the Word made flesh. Therefore when Jesus wakes up in the morning he comes into consciousness with an intuitive, personal grasp of this. He is present to himself in plain and simple self-awareness as the person who he is. At

the transcendental pole he has this subjective self-knowledge.
But it takes his whole lifetime for him to spell this out in clear
categories, in clear terms. It takes the experiences of his ministry, of those who reject him and those who accept him, of
those who go up and ask him, "Are you the Christ?" and so
on. It takes his whole life for him to understand himself in
concrete terms. In other words, when Jesus woke up in the
morning, he did not begin the day saying "I am the Word
made flesh." Rather, he came into consciousness as Jesus of
Nazareth and became aware of who he was in the concrete
through the course of his life as does everyone else.

Remember that when Jesus did express himself in objective
terms, he did so in Jewish and not in Greek categories. We are
dealing here with a human being who was a first-century Jew
using the thought patterns of his own people. Obviously, Jesus
did not wake up in the morning saying "I am the Son of God
with a truly human nature and a truly divine nature that come
together in one hypostatis." I do not know what he said in the
morning, but we can be virtually certain it was not that! Jesus
did not have at hand the full-blown doctrine of the later
church about himself. He came into consciousness at the
subjective level and operated out of a deep sense of himself as
the person he is, but it took his life experiences to spell that
out into adequate terms. As with all of us, the mystery of his
person was never totally expressed in concrete terms up until
the time of his death, when he transcends this world and is
raised from the dead. Then his ultimate identity burst upon
him in all clarity. This is not to say that all along he did not
have a sense of who he was at the subjective level, just as all
through our life we have a sense of who we are and act on it.
But for Jesus as for ourselves, experiences help us grow in
concrete awareness.

Let us meditate on how this works out in practical terms.
When Jesus was a baby, he knew no more than any other baby
would know, e.g., that he was cold or hungry or wet or

whatever. As a toddler he learned from his parents the things he needed to know—how to walk, how to talk. In the pattern of Jewish boys of the day, he would have been sent to school in the synagogue to learn how to read and write, and to study Torah. (In his adult life Jesus is obviously literate, reading the scroll of Isaiah in the synagogue [Lk 4:16-20] and writing those mysterious words on the ground in front of the woman taken in adultery [Jn 8:1–11]). He grew up in a particular religious Jewish household. This approach opens up a great deal of room for reflection on the influence of Mary and Joseph on Jesus. He obviously developed in a very loving, free, religious home, judging from the patterns of behavior he exhibits in his adult ministry.

At the age of twelve, there is the interesting scene in the temple when Jesus gets lost from his parents for three days. What we have here, in the view of some biblical exegetes, is an intelligent boy discovering his vocation. This country boy who grew up in the hill country comes for the first time into the big city. There he is taken with the magnificence of the temple (there was only one temple in the whole country), with its many courtyards, its music, incense, priestly liturgies and sacrifices. A deep chord is struck. The things of God attract and fascinate him, and so he stays behind. When his parents find him, he is sitting among the teachers, "listening to them and asking them questions." He is a boy with these tremendous questions about God and religious matters. And all who heard him, Luke goes on, "were amazed at his understanding and his answers." Already at a young age Jesus has a great deal of wisdom about religious matters and is trying to find out more from those who really are the religious teachers. His response to his parents bears this out—his Father's house is where his heart is (Lk 2:42–50).

After that scene Jesus disappears for many, many years, the hidden years of Nazareth. Not knowing what went on there, we presume that he learned carpentry from Joseph and eventually took over the carpenter's business. No doubt he passed those years as an observant Jew, going to Jerusalem for the feasts, praying the daily prayers. What was the one event in his adult life which set him on the path to his own public ministry? All four gospels agree that it was the preaching of John the Baptist. Along with many others, Jesus went out to listen to him, eventually stepping forward to receive John's baptism. This is a significant religious moment, and the gospels use images such as a voice from heaven and a dove descending to signify the revelation of his vocation. After that his life changed. He went to the desert to prepare and fast, and then started to preach. Later Jesus was to say about John the Baptist that no one born of woman was greater than he. It becomes very clear that John was influential on Jesus, modeling for him the pattern of a prophet. Jesus will be very different from John, announcing salvation rather than doom. Nevertheless, there is a tremendous amount of mutual respect between these two prophets, if not their followers.

In his ministry Jesus evidenced an extraordinary sense of his own mission. Where did this come from? He was a layman in his own day, not a priest, not a trained teacher. He had no credentials to do what he did—no diploma hung on his wall. He was a simple worker, a carpenter, possessed by the Spirit of God to proclaim the word of God with authority. The people recognized the authenticity of his teaching. Where did he get the power to speak this way? There is a sense in Jesus of his own mission, his own authority, his own strong self. He reaches out to the poorest and the most dispossessed of persons. He dares to call God the child-like name "Abba." Where does this come from? In the light of our previous analysis, we would say that it wells up from the subjective pole of his own self-awareness, where he intuits who he is, utterly related to God. There is a great deal in his ministry that can be explained this way.

At the same time, Jesus needs to think about things, to

pray, to struggle, and to make decisions amid the uncertainties of his itinerant ministry. It is clear that some people helped him to understand his ministry, challenged him, encouraged him. Toward the end of his life Jesus had a sense of death approaching, for threats were made on his life; he was warned not to go to Jerusalem, etc. In fidelity to his Father's will he decided in the end to go and preach the word of God in the heart of the capital city itself during the feast. It was a dangerous decision, but he stayed the course. After giving his disciples a memorial of himself in bread and wine, he prayed in the olive garden, still struggling: "Father, if it is possible, let this chalice pass from me." He did not want to die but was hoping against hope that this would not be his fate. Yet, "not my will but Thine be done" (Mk 14:36). If Jesus had run away from the garden while he still had time, if he had gone back and opened up the carpenter's shop, he might have lived to a ripe old age. He still had choices to make, and his choice in the end was to be faithful to the love in his heart, to his God, to himself. Thus he remained steadfast in his mission. Ultimately he was arrested and tortured and executed by the state. On the cross he experienced an abandonment by God, a sense that God was absent, and died crying out loud (Mk 15:37). Where was God at the very end? Jesus died handing himself over to God even while feeling the absence of God, uttering his last words to God who seemed not to hear. As we trace it historically, even at that last moment of his death Jesus did not have, at the categorical level, a full concrete grasp of everything about himself. For this, it would take the resurrection.

Conclusion

Let us conclude by considering this question: Did Jesus know he was God, yes or no? In the light of what we have developed here, the answer is both yes and no. Yes, at the

subjective level; Jesus is who he is and has the intuitive knowledge of that. No, at the objective level; he had to grow con-
cretely into that knowledge in the course of his lifetime up to
the end. In other words, he knew who he was implicitly but
not in clear terms and in clear concepts. Consider this same
question in a more historical way. Did this first-century Jewish
man think he was Yahweh? No; for a first-century Jew to
think he was Yahweh would have been either idolatrous or a
little crazy. Before Jesus could be professed as God by Christian believers, our very idea of God had to undergo transformation into trinitarian form. Another way to consider this
question: When Jesus prayed, was he talking to himself? No;
he was praying to Yahweh, the God of Israel, whom he called
Abba. In the clear words and concepts of categorical knowledge, he was not thinking of himself in divine terms. Always
being the Messiah, he grew into a clear grasp of his own
messiahship during his lifetime. What the church did in the
decades after the crucifixion and resurrection, and certainly in
the centuries of the early councils, was to make explicit what
is implicit already in the person and the ministry of Jesus. The
church drew this out into doctrines. But during his lifetime,
Jesus himself did not have the benefit of later reflection about
himself. In fact what necessarily informs Christian perception
of his identity is the resurrection. Until that had happened
there was still another piece of evidence that had to come in
before a full confession of who he is could have taken place.
This is a historical approach, obviously giving room in history for Jesus' own true humanity to function, even psycholog-
ically.

In conclusion let us ponder a point made by Cyril of
Alexandria, a bishop and theologian who was a very strong
defender of the divinity of Christ: "We have admired his
goodness in that for love of us he has not refused to descend to
such a low position as to bear all that belongs to our nature,
included in which is ignorance." Cyril is encouraging us to be

realistic about this ignorance, because it is an acid test of the incarnation. Do we really believe that God has loved us so much as to identify with everything in our human life including ignorance? If so, we are glimpsing the depths of God's self-emptying in the incarnation. The bipolar way of understanding human self-knowledge is simply a theological construct that perhaps can help us think about how such self-emptying is possible.

Readings

The state of the question in Catholic theology before the biblical renewal triggered by Vatican II is beautifully illustrated by Romano Guardini, *The Humanity of Christ: Contributions to a Psychology of Jesus* (New York: Pantheon Books, 1964); see also Karl Adam, *The Christ of Faith* (above, chap. 1).

Critical biblical background for this question is well presented by Raymond Brown, "How Much Did Jesus Know?" *Jesus—God and Man* (Milwaukee: Bruce Pub., 1967), 39–102. James Dunn, *Jesus and the Spirit* (Philadelphia: Westminster, 1975), explores New Testament texts which reflect Jesus' human religious experience, and in *The Evidence for Jesus* (Philadelphia: Westminster, 1985) takes up the thorny question of Jesus' self-consciousness as Son of God, again from a biblical viewpoint.

Rahner's key to unraveling the tension between biblical and theological traditions over this issue is presented in "Dogmatic Reflections on the Knowledge and Self-Consciousness of Christ," *Theological Investigations* 5: 193–215. For a different approach to the same problematic, see Bernard Lonergan, "Christ as Subject: A Reply," *Collection I,* Frederick Crowe, ed. (New York: Herder & Herder, 1967).

4

The History of Jesus

Within a highly structured dogmatic framework, the first wave of renewal in Catholic christology occurred in the 1950's and 1960's when theologians pondered the dogmatic confession of Jesus Christ's identity. The insights that emerged pointed to a deeper appreciation of the genuine humanity of the Word made flesh, and of the dignity and value of every human being. The Second Vatican Council incorporated the results of much of this work and built on it. The council also took a step that was to be highly significant for developments in christology, namely, it approved the study of the scriptures using modern historical and critical methods. As a result, Catholic biblical scholarship came into its own, and the gospels began to be studied as never before.

The second wave of renewal in Catholic christology formed and swelled as a direct result. Theologians now began christology by reflecting not on the Chalcedonian dogma but on the scriptural stories and testimony about Jesus Christ, leading to ideas which have a concrete and historical flavor to them. The questions which now arise concern not his human nature, divine nature, and one hypostasis, but his life's story: What was he like as a real person in history? What did he stand for? How did he make such an impact? Why did the authorities consider him dangerous? Why was he crucified?

Starting in the late 1960's and flowering in the 1970's this

approach was followed by theologians such as Karl Rahner in
his later years, Edward Schillebeeckx (still working on the
third volume of his trilogy on Jesus Christ), Hans Küng,
Walter Kasper, Gerald O'Collins, James Mackey, Monika
Hellwig, William Thompson, and many others. The guiding
motivation of their work springs from Christian faith with a
turn to the practical. If God became a human being, and this
is what the first wave of renewal emphasized, then it is very
important to see what kind of human being God became. If
Jesus is God with us, then his story is an answer to the
question, "Who is God?" If Jesus is the revelation of God and
stood for definite purposes and upheld certain values, then the
significance of that for believers is inestimable. What he does,
in the concrete, matters; it embodies the way of God in this
world which patterns our way as disciples today. In other
words, Jesus does not just have a human nature in the abstract, but a very concrete human history. We need to put *that*
story into dialogue with our own lives today.

What results is a narrative christology. Its method is to
uncover the story of Jesus in history and then to correlate this
story with the situation of the community of disciples today.
When contemporary biblical scholarship studies the gospels,
what emerges as of first-rate importance is the ministry of
Jesus. It is interesting that for centuries Catholic christology
did not deal with Jesus' adult activities very extensively, but
focused its attention on his birth and death. If you doubt this,
just think of the traditional mysteries of the Rosary, where
meditation skips from the joyful to the sorrowful mysteries
without lingering over what happened in between. The second
wave of renewal has recovered the historical ministry as intrinsically important to christology.

There is a shift taking place here, from a christology "from
above" to a christology "from below." In John's gospel, in
patristic and medieval christology, as well as in the first wave of
renewal which grappled with the dogma about Jesus Christ,

thought begins in heaven, "above." Starting with the belief that this is the Word of God, we trace his descent into our world, marveling at the love of God which impels such identification with us and our troubles. In the christology of the synoptic gospels (Matthew, Mark, and Luke), as well as in this second wave of renewal which seeks to tell the story of Jesus, thought begins on earth, "below." Starting with the concrete memories of Jesus of Nazareth and his impact, we trace his ascent through death and resurrection to the glory of God, challenged to follow his way in our own lives as a believing community. In this approach, Jesus is named first of all a prophet and messenger from God—and more than a prophet; the greatest of the prophets; the eschatological prophet who brings the final word from God into the world, a word of compassionate and liberating love.

Thinking about Jesus Christ first of all from the scriptures has led to a practical, narrative christology which places the story of Jesus in critical correlation with the lives of believers today. The story involves three moments: ministry, death, resurrection. The ministry in turn is comprised of three elements: his preaching, characteristic way of behaving, and manner of relating to God. Finally, the correlation takes place in three ways, as the church believes, acts, and theorizes upon the story of Jesus.

Ministry: Preaching

Jesus was an inspired preacher, filled with the Holy Spirit. The word of God burned in him and attracted others as he proclaimed it. What did he preach? His focus was not on extended doctrines, or on himself, his significance and identity. Rather, at the heart of his preaching was the symbol of the reign of God. Taken from the Hebrew tradition this symbol signifies what the state of affairs will be when God is recognized as the One on whom everyone sets their hearts, when

God finally reigns. The kingdom of God is *God* getting the divine way unopposed by human sinfulness and the powers of darkness. On that day everyone will do what God wants, the will of God will be done on earth. In the Lord's Prayer we say, "Thy kingdom come, Thy will be done on earth as it is in heaven," and we are asking for the same thing in two different ways. The reign of God is the situation that results when God's will is really done. What is God's will? As revealed in Jesus, God's will is our well-being. God wants the wholeness, the healing, and the salvation of every creature and of all of us taken together. The reign of God, then, involves justice and peace among everyone, healing and wholeness everywhere, fullness of life enjoyed by all. It is what the scriptures call the situation of *shalom,* peace experienced not only as the absence of war but peace as the fullness of life. God wills this to come, God wants the world to be this way. In the prophets there are many beautiful images which evoke this reign of God: the lion lying down with the lamb (the strong not eating up the weak); soldiers beating war instruments into farming instruments; a marvelous harvest; a wedding feast with food enough for everyone and joy all around. All of these images could be supplemented by pictures of life today. What would the reign of God be like in urban images, in images taken from life in the United States, in Central American images, in Palestinian images, in South African images? What values would prevail? It is a reign of justice and peace, the fullness of life for every single person.

Jesus' preaching was shaped by the tradition of Judaism which was hoping for the reign of God, expecting that the reign of God would come at the last day when God came to judge the living and the dead and set up the kingdom of justice and peace. A new and burning sense that this reign is *near* pervades his preaching. The first words out of his mouth in Mark's gospel proclaim, "The time has come; the kingdom is near. Repent and believe in the good news" (Mk 1:15).

What Jesus is announcing is that we do not have to wait until the last day for *shalom* to arrive, but God is already drawing near with salvation for all. It is dawning, it is breaking in, it is already starting to happen. The reign of God is at hand; salvation is on its way from God. This message is very urgent. There is an excitement about Jesus' preaching, a sense of anticipation as God approaches to heal and to save. And what must we do? Repent and believe in the good news. Turn our hearts around, open up, be converted, and believe the good news. This *is* good news if it is true. It is great news that the reign of God is near instead of far away on the last day. I have sometimes asked my students, "What is good about the good news?" And I have not often received much of an answer, because religion seems kind of grim and dutiful and serious. It is anything but that in the preaching of Jesus. The symbol of the reign of God flowers in his imagination as the good news that God, powerful and compassionate, is coming close and wills to save, to establish justice and peace for all. This is what Jesus preaches in hundreds of different ways. Many of his parables begin, "the reign of God is like"; as the stories unfold, there is always a twist somewhere that leaves us wondering. The parables show that the reign of God is going to be surprising; it is not going to involve business as usual. Values are going to be turned upside down, and people whom the world considered nonpersons will be first, brought especially into the center of the kingdom. This is indeed good news if you are one of the last, least, or lowest! The beatitudes of Jesus also reflect this: Blessed are the poor, those who mourn, those who hunger and thirst for justice, those who make peace, because theirs is the kingdom of heaven (Mt 5:3–12).

This message of the reign of God comes with a great challenge for those who will not repent and believe the good news. Woe to the rich, the overstuffed, the esteemed, to those who think they deserve the front seats, to those who oppress and bind heavy burdens on the back of the poor. When the reign of God comes, they are going to be cast out—unless they repent. This message has teeth in it; it is not all sweetness and light. There is always the option to repent, but it is a challenge to those who think they have got it made to open their minds and hearts and enter into the perspective of God toward the oppressed. The reign of justice and peace, the reign of *shalom,* the reign of God—this marvelous hope is at the heart of all of Jesus' preaching. He is possessed with it and its nearness.

Ministry: Characteristic Behavior

Jesus did not just speak about the coming reign of God. In his own practical ways he enacted it. In the things he did it began to arrive, began to come about in people's lives. What kind of behavior was characteristic of him?

1. Jesus called disciples to follow him. Women as well as men responded, leaving their families, their homes, their jobs, and their villages. They formed a community of brothers and sisters around him, traveling with him, listening to him and being taught by him, learning his ways and even being sent on mission by him, little trial runs into ministry while he was still with them. After Jesus' death and resurrection, this band of followers formed the nucleus of the church.

2. He showed partisanship for the marginal people of his society and did so in many, many ways. He associated with sinners, offering them forgiveness. He frequently healed the sick, reaching out to touch them, and disputing the belief that sickness was a punishment for sin. By the power of God working through him Jesus restored *shalom* to their bodies and to their spirits. In the case of lepers and others whose sickness had ostracized them from the community, his cures brought them back into life-giving relationships with other human beings. Jesus also exorcised demons, struggling with the power of evil; again, through him the power of God overcame evil and brought the afflicted back into harmony

with God, with their own spirits, and so with others. Over and over again, Jesus typically searched for and reached out to the marginal lives of his society, to people suffering physically, spiritually, and socially, giving them a taste of the joy of the kingdom's arrival. In a particular way, his ministry shows the triumph of God's will over the forces that bind people who are considered of no account.

3. Jesus shared companionship both with his disciples and with the wider circle of those interested in him. Religious art has focused on the Last Supper, but indeed it was only the last of a whole history of suppers that Jesus had with "his own" and with others. In the culture of the Middle East, sitting down at table with someone and breaking bread sets up a real bond of kinship. Not done lightly, this action makes people into friends, colleagues, "family." What Jesus did was to sit down at table with all manner of folks, including sinners, tax collectors, prostitutes, people considered nonentities and out-side the reign of God in every way. They would break bread together after his preaching, after many people had been healed and forgiven, celebrating their return to one another. People found themselves at the table with Jesus in a new kind of community, sharing with people they never thought they would sit down with. A foretaste of the kingdom of God is savored at these joyful meals, where Jesus is guest of honor or host. No doubt the wine flowed freely at these suppers, for Jesus is accused by the Pharisees of being a drunk and a glutton. In addition his disciples are criticized for not fasting as did John the Baptist's. This was a genuine historical crit-icism that stung. Not that Jesus was guilty as charged. But he was perceived as someone who made merry, and his meals were considered a bit uproarious, very joyful, a foretaste of the joy of the kingdom in its fullness. Edward Schillebeeckx, who deals at length with these suppers, makes an interesting point: At these meals, being sad in Jesus' presence is an existential impossibility. You just could not keep your own sadness in

that kind of company. The reign of God is near, Jesus is its mediator, and as you get into his circle, the joy breaks out. This is not a superficial joy. It springs from a deep sense that persons are restored to their own dignity and peace before God, and there find themselves in a new community with one another. It is a foretaste of the kingdom of God.

4. Jesus is both faithful and free regarding the great Jewish tradition of Torah. Raised in a religious household and taught to observe the Jewish customs and to pray the Jewish prayers, Jesus was a Jew, an observant Jew. But there were occasions when he broke the Torah, and that gave scandal. In every single case when the law was set aside, it was because the well-being of someone was at stake. In face of the sick, the suffering, and the hungry, the sabbath observances were given second priority. That is how he interprets the Torah. When challenged as to what was the greatest commandment among the many of the Torah, his fundamental answer was to lift up two of them and make them one: "You shall love the Lord your God with all your heart and soul and mind and strength; and you shall love your neighbour as yourself" (Mt 22:37–39). In other words love is at the heart of the reign of God; not an easy love but a self-giving love on the model of God. Such love grounds the law, puts it in correct perspective, and fulfills it. Loving this way, Jesus himself creates a liberating life-style and shows a wonderful freedom to do good.

5. It is very clear in the gospels that Jesus' whole ministry was rooted in prayer. In addition to the prescribed daily and feast-day Jewish prayers, Jesus also prayed with personal initiative. He would go out at night by himself to pray. He would also find time for his disciples to come away from the crowds now and then to reflect. He even taught them how to pray for the coming of God's reign. Running throughout his ministry was a very deep spirituality as source of the preaching and effective action in which he was involved.

Ministry: Relationship to God

From the way Jesus talked about God and enacted the reign of God, it is obvious that he had a special and original experience of God as intimate, close, and tremendously compassionate over human suffering and sin. Out of that experience Jesus surfaced a name for God, namely *Abba*. In the Hebrew scriptures God is occasionally called "Father" in some of the psalms and prophets. But *Abba* does not exactly mean Father. It is the Aramaic word that a small child would use to address his or her father before being able to talk. As such a babble word, it really translates into English as "papa" or "dada" or some other equivalent. Every language has these little words that children use before they can really speak, but which they can use to call on their nearest and dearest. Jesus' own personal experience of God as close and compassionate led him to name God in this very intimate way, *Abba*. The name evokes the power of a very close relationship between Jesus and the One he names this way. Furthermore, Jesus teaches others to call God *Abba,* encouraging them to trust God the way little children trust a good parent to take care of them, be compassionate over their weakness, and stand guard against those who would harm them. Jesus' *Abba* experience is the heart of the matter, the dynamism behind his preaching the reign of God and of his typical way of acting. God *Abba* was the passion of his life.

Death

In this historical approach, it becomes crystal clear that Jesus' death was not an accident. Rather, it was the price he paid for his ministry. First of all, Jesus triggered a great deal of conflict with the religious authorities of his day. He did not necessarily want this, but it was almost inevitable, given the

preaching and activity that he was engaged in. He was stand-
ing for one interpretation of God and Torah in the face of
another more official interpretation that was held by the religious leaders. The Jewish tradition came into conflict with
itself. There was also a sense among these leaders, especially
evident in some of the trial scenes, that the enthusiasm generated by Jesus' ministry was dangerous in a political sense.
Crowds of people were following him and there could easily
be an uprising, which would cause the Romans, the occupying
military power, to devastate the land. Recall that famous scene
where the high priest says it is better that one man should die
for the people than that the Romans should come and burn all
the cities (Jn 11:48–50). Thus, the leaders rejected him for
religious reasons, actually accusing him during his trial of
blasphemy, of claiming the authority to understand God better than the governing religious leaders themselves did. But
they also worried about the political implication of his ministry and where that would lead, and decided they could not
afford to leave him at large. In the face of that opposition,
Jesus went ahead with his ministry, continuing freely in love,
commitment, and fidelity; if he had chosen to opt out of his
ministry he would not necessarily have ended up crucified.
Events then took their rapid course. He was arrested, interro-
gated, tortured, and put to death. Historically, he died a
failure. His message was rejected by many people; among his
disciples one betrayed him, one denied even knowing him,
most of the males abandoned him, although the women kept
vigil at the cross; his ministry came to a screeching halt. He
was executed in the prime of his life.

Worst of all, it seemed that even God, whom he had
preached as compassionate and loving *Abba,* had abandoned
him. Where was God? What kind of God would let this
happen to such a faithful servant? Jesus on the cross cried out
the opening line of Psalm 22, "My God, My God, why have
you forsaken me?" expressing what one suspects is a real

experience of the absence of God in the midst of suffering. If Jesus indeed had a last temptation, I suspect that its direction lay here, in the invitation to despair of the faithfulness of *Abba.* Yet he persisted in calling out to God, and this psalm does end on a note of hope that God will deliver the one who is suffering. Not withstanding this, in its own context the cross itself was not a holy event, as we think of the sacred in our stereotypical way. It was a civil execution; it was gruesome. Charged with a political crime, that of being king of the Jews, or a messianic pretender, Jesus died perceived by others to be wrong. He was one more troublesome upstart, dead between two others who were thieves. Nothing sacred about that. The depth of the sin of this world is reflected there on the cross.

Very early on, believers had the insight that after he died, Jesus descended into hell; we still confess this in the Creed. What does this mean? Jesus has gone down into the realm of the dead, to *Sheol,* the kingdom of shadows. What this symbolic way of speaking signifies is that even those who die victimized, those who disappear, those who are no longer part of the living history of the earth, those no longer remembered—all these people are not beyond the reach of the living God. The crucified Jesus has joined them, identifying with them, and bringing the power of the reign of God even there.

Resurrection

The story does not end here. Early in the morning two days later Mary Magdalene and other women disciples went to the tomb with oils for a last anointing of Jesus' body. Instead of a corpse they encountered the living Christ and bore witness of this to the other disciples. As events raced on the conviction of faith rose up: The raising of the dead which was supposed to happen on the last day with the coming of the reign of God has already begun to happen. By the loving power of God

Jesus is transformed into glory, he is raised up. Such existence is beyond our imagination, for it is life in another dimension beyond the limits of time and space; it is life in the dimension of God. It is better symbolized in the Easter Vigil liturgy, with its dramatic scenes of light out of darkness, proclamation of the creation story, sprinkling the water of new life, and sharing the eucharistic bread. Rather than coming to nothing in death, Jesus died into God. He is risen, whole and entire, as the embodied person he was in this life—his wounds are a sign of that.

If Jesus Christ is not risen, then our faith is in vain, and of all people we are stupid and most to be pitied (1 Cor 15:17–19). Everything depends upon this! First of all, God is revealed as really being the way that Jesus had preached. God is *Abba*, on the side of the one rejected, able to give a future to someone who has none. Henceforth, we can trust God to have the last word on our behalf, as indeed God had the first, and that word is *life*. In addition, the resurrection vindicates Jesus' message, ministry, even his person. He had been found guilty by human judges, who did away with him as a danger to religious tradition and the stability of the state. God now overturns the judgment of those judges and says there is another, divine judgment to be made about this crucified criminal, namely, that he is the Son of God. Finally, a future of hope opens up for every human being and for the whole of creation. If God has so raised Jesus, then that same future becomes a real possibility and hope for the rest of us. "A piece of this earth, real to the core, is now forever with God in glory" . . . and the final *shalom* has broken into this world not just as a possibility but as a real beginning.

The overriding consideration in a christology "from below" is that the resurrection happened not just to anyone but to the Crucified One. And Jesus was not crucified by accident but because of the kind of ministry he persisted in carrying out. Thus the ministry interprets the death as well as the resurrec-

tion, giving us a concrete picture of precisely who was vindi-
cated in the resurrection. It is the Jesus of the ministry who
was shown to be Son of God in power through the resurrection—and this is the one whom disciples follow.

Correlation with the Community of Disciples

Bringing the story of Jesus into critical correlation with the
lives of believers today involves us not just with our private
selves but with the whole church and the community of the
whole world. As the early disciples, after the resurrection and
the outpouring of the Holy Spirit, preached and witnessed to
Jesus Christ, giving him names out of their cultural contexts,
so too today. Disciples are still inspired by the power of the
Holy Spirit and, guided by the tradition generated through
the experiences of the early communities, should be engaged
in active following, in writing the fifth gospel so to speak.
There are three moments in a living christology done this way
in response to what is given by God in the story of Jesus.

1. Telling the story. As a community the church is a story-
telling group of people, telling the story of Jesus as the story of
God with us. The church does in fact tell this story: Parents
tell it to their children, catechists tell it, preachers tell it. At
every Eucharist we also tell it, first at the reading of the gospel,
and then at the very heart of the eucharistic prayer when
language slips into a narrative mode and recounts how "on
the night before he died, he took bread . . ." The story of his
self-giving is at the center of our praise and thanks to God. We
are a story-telling people! Particularly effective in illuminating
the power of the story is a tale told by Martin Buber.

A rabbi related the following: "My grandfather was para-
lyzed. One day he was asked to tell about something that
happened with his teacher, the great Balshem. Then he told
how this saintly Balshem used to leap about and dance while
he was at his prayers. As he went on with the story my

grandfather stood up: he was so carried away that he had to show how the master had done it and he started to caper about dancing. From that moment he was cured."

Says Buber, *that* is how stories should be told. We add, *that* is how the story of Jesus should be told, so we become what we tell in the telling. It is a transformative telling. It is a telling that makes Jesus alive and present, transforming us into persons of love and witness.

2. Living the story. The church is called to put its feet in the footsteps of Jesus and walk the way that he walked. If he is the Way, the Truth, and the Life then his way must be our way. If he stood for compassionate love then so should the church. If he reached out to the most marginal people, then according to changing circumstances, so should the church. In fact only if we are in solidarity with him, who is in solidarity with God, who is in solidarity with those who suffer, will any christology be credible, especially in this world which is crying out for justice. The overriding importance of praxis leads some theologians such as Schillebeeckx to question whether "Who do you say that I am" with its resulting theoretical speculation is in fact the best way to pose the christological question today. It may well be more fruitful for Jesus Christ to be asking today "How have you been committed to the reign of God?" and to let our answer to the question of his meaning be shaped by our action on behalf of justice. In other words, the church must be about the business of the reign of God in order for its thought about Jesus Christ to be true.

3. Theorizing about the story. In the midst of telling the story and living the story, we also engage in the classical activity of theorizing about it, but here theologians tend to be more reticent than in the past. We cannot define, ultimately, the mystery of the person of Jesus, the mystery of the suffering of the cross, the mystery of the victorious love of God that breaks through in the midst of it all. We are dealing here with the very depth of our faith. We can make affirmations about

Jesus but we cannot grasp him in our concepts. Suggestions have been made for reformulating the insights of the early councils. Would it be possible to rephrase Chalcedon in the terminology of our day and say, Jesus is in total solidarity with God (divine nature); Jesus is in total solidarity with us (human nature); and both of these solidarities form who he is and constitutes his person (one person)? This is one of Schillebeeckx's proposals, and open to discussion. Again, could we express the idea that Jesus is the Word of God in a more contemporary idiom by saying that he is the parable of God? He did not just tell parables but he *is* the story that God is telling in the world. Instead of giving Jesus more exalted titles, could we simply say that Jesus is God's great No to suffering and God's great Yes to laughter? He did not bring joy in a superficial way but by entering into suffering on the cross and triumphing over it in the resurrection. These are some of the theorizings that have come up in this narrative approach. To date this christology has been rich in images and weak in metaphysics. The interest has been not so much on philosophical analysis of Jesus' inner constitution as in practical fidelity to this history. As church we are called to tell the story of Jesus, recall his dangerous memory, walk in his footsteps and, in the power of the Spirit, struggle against the forces of death. These actions will shape a practical, living christology in our own time.

Readings

Catholic theology came late to the quest for the historical Jesus. One of the loveliest early Protestant influences upon its own questing is Günther Bornkamm, *Jesus of Nazareth* (New York: Harper & Row, 1960). A synthesis of biblical materials from the Catholic viewpoint is shaped by Donald Senior, *Jesus, a Gospel Portrait* (Dayton, OH: Pflaum Press, 1975); and by Gerard Sloyan, *Jesus in Focus: A Life in Its Setting* (Mystic, CN: Twenty-Third Pubns.,

1983). Biblical data is presented in simple, pithy form in Joseph Fitzmyer, *A Christological Catechism: New Testament Answers* (New York: Paulist, 1982), which includes a translation of the official instruction of the Pontifical Biblical Commission "On The Historical Truth of the Gospels."

Insofar as the historical approach realizes the catastrophe occasioned by Jesus' death, it places particular emphasis on the resurrection. Helpful biblical and theological reflections on this event/mystery are Gerald O'Collins, *The Resurrection of Jesus Christ* (London: Darton, Longman and Todd, 1973); Raymond Brown, *The Virginal Conception and the Bodily Resurrection of Jesus* (New York: Paulist, 1978); Pheme Perkins, *Resurrection: New Testament Witness and Contemporary Reflection* (Garden City, NY: Doubleday, 1984); and Jerome Neyrey, *The Resurrection Stories* (Wilmington, DL: Glazier, 1988).

Bringing understandings of Jesus' own history into new frameworks of christology continues to absorb great attention. The most masterful work to date has been that of Edward Schillebeeckx's two volumes: *Jesus: An Experiment in Christology* (New York: Seabury, 1979), and *Christ: The Experience of Jesus as Lord* (New York: Seabury, 1980). More accessible and readable are his meditative pieces on Jesus Christ, *God Among Us: The Gospel Proclaimed* (New York: Crossroad, 1983). The mind of this theologian is illuminated by a series of introductory essays in Robert Schreiter and Mary Catherine Hilkert, eds., *The Praxis of Christian Experience* (San Francisco: Harper & Row, 1989).

A number of other theologians have made extensive use of biblical historical material in thinking about Jesus Christ. Some of the best include Hans Küng, *On Being A Christian* (Garden City, NY: Doubleday, 1976); Walter Kasper, *Jesus the Christ* (New York: Paulist, 1976); Dermot Lane, *The Reality of Jesus* (New York: Paulist, 1975); James Mackey, *Jesus, The Man and the Myth* (New York: Paulist, 1979); Gerald O'Collins, *Interpreting Jesus* (New York: Paulist, 1983); and Monika Hellwig, *Jesus the Compassion of God* (Wilmington, DL: Glazier, 1983). The foundational moves of several of these authors are studied in Robert Krieg, *Story-Shaped Christology: The Role of Narratives in Identifying Jesus Christ* (New York: Paulist, 1988).

One new area opened up by this approach is the Jewishness of Jesus. Anthony Tambasco provides a very readable account of how Jesus was part of Judaism and how he moved beyond it in *In the Days of Jesus: The Jewish Background and Unique Teaching of Jesus* (New York: Paulist, 1983). A critical presentation of Jesus' relation to his culture is E.P. Sanders, *Jesus and Judaism* (Philadelphia: Fortress, 1985). Religious implications are spelled out in Leonard Swidler, *Yeshua: A Model for Moderns* (Kansas City, MO: Sheed & Ward, 1988). From the Jewish perspective, interesting insights are presented by Samuel Sandmel, *We Jews and Jesus* (New York: Oxford University Press, 1965); and Géza Vermès, *Jesus the Jew* (Philadelphia: Fortress, 1981).

The value of this historical approach for preaching and theology becomes clear in Leander Keck, *A Future for the Historical Jesus* (London: SCM Press, 1972); and its strategic use in an important contemporary controversy is delineated by Stanley Marrow, *The Words of Jesus in Our Gospels: A Catholic Response to Fundamentalism* (New York: Paulist, 1979).

5

Jesus Christ and Justice

The first wave of renewal in christology has sculptured a new landscape by removing the church's forgetfulness of the genuine humanity of God with us. As a result, the incarnation is appreciated as a much more startling event than when it simply involved the union of God with a quasi-humanity. The second wave has chiseled the human features of the historical Jesus in bold relief, giving the church's memory of Jesus a new and compelling concreteness. Neither of these movements has taken place in a vacuum, which is a misimpression that may be created when they are singled out by themselves for close scrutiny. Rather, the pressing needs of our age coupled with the character of post-Vatican II theology turned toward the troubled world have led christology into immediate contact with issues of discipleship, that is, the following of Jesus Christ. The question about who we say he is invites an answer in practical living as well as in reflection. Furthermore, the practical concerns of today reach beyond the personal and the interpersonal to include the structural and cosmic, and rightly so if the victory over the "powers and principalities" won in the crucified Jesus is significant for the whole universe and not just for individuals in isolation.

What is the dynamism of our faith confession in Jesus Christ that generates action on behalf of justice as a constitutive element of that faith? What is this relation between christology and social justice that is emerging as a new insight in the Christian imagination of our time?

As soon as we begin to analyze this relation, it becomes more complex due to the pluralism existing in theology today. Similar to the situation in the first century, when a diversity of cultural experiences led different Christian communities to articulate Jesus' significance in various ways, giving us the diverse christologies of Paul, Mark, and John, the church today as an emerging world church is witnessing diverse christologies born from the experience of believers on different continents. To find a path through this pluralism, and to get to the heart of the question about christology's relation to social justice, we can borrow a page from Karl Rahner. According to his analysis, all christologies can in the end be characterized as belonging to one of two basic types: a salvation history or ascending type, commonly called christology from below, and a metaphysical or descending type, commonly called christology from above. The two are not mutually exclusive, and the Church needs both for the full confession of its faith. They are distinct, however, bringing into play different scriptural and doctrinal emphases and a different method of thinking.

To illustrate the unbreakable relation between Jesus Christ and social justice in each of these patterns of thinking, we may turn to key teachings of church leaders. This in itself highlights one aspect of the dynamic of a living tradition, namely, once a ferment in theological development reaches a certain stage of maturity, its tested insights begin to be used in common parlance of the teaching of the church. Thus they are preserved and handed on to future generations.

The first wave of christological renewal is clearly present in the first encyclical of John Paul II on Jesus Christ as redeemer of the human race. There he presents a descending type of christology focused primarily on Jesus Christ's redemptive incarnation and its healing effect on the whole human race.

His argument stands or falls on the reality of the genuine humanity of Jesus, for by that humanity Jesus is united to every other human being, gifting each of us with a dignity beyond compare which mandates justice for all. On the other hand, the second wave of renewal in christology shapes the pastoral letters on peacemaking and economic justice written by the United States Catholic bishops. In these teaching letters the bishops delineate an ascending type of christology which draws its inspiration from the ministry of the earthly Jesus, culminating in his death and resurrection. Without the concrete example of Jesus and the values enunciated in his preaching, the bishops' case loses its persuasive Christian power. While following different trains of thought, however, both approaches are one in appealing to the intrinsic dynamism of the question "Who do you say that I am?" which sets believers to following the way of Jesus Christ in care and commitment for the suffering neighbor, and in critique and change of the systems which cause that suffering. Uncovering the logic of their different arguments shows that both propel the church in the same direction, from the foundation of confessing faith in Jesus Christ to the challenge of action on behalf of justice.

Descending Christology

This type of christology has been the predominant one in the course of the Christian tradition. It begins its thinking in heaven with the doctrine of the Second Person of the Blessed Trinity, the Word of God preexisting from all eternity in unity with the Father and the Spirit. As its name suggests, this christology then traces the descent of the eternal Word into this world, fascinated with the mystery of the incarnation, the Word become flesh. The one through whom all things were made is now in the world under the conditions of sin and alienation, in order to renew creation which God has never ceased to love. As the Incarnate Word, Jesus Christ reveals the love and mercy of God and, through his identification with human existence culminating in the cross and resurrection, restores human beings to their likeness to God which had been disfigured by sin. Indeed, the whole cosmos is redeemed and made into a new creation. Thus the genuine descent of the eternal Word into human existence is a redemptive event par excellence; Jesus Christ's metaphysical identity is the ground of his function as Redeemer of the human race. This pattern of christology finds its scriptural paradigm in the gospel of John: "In the beginning was the Word, and the Word was with God, and the Word was God . . . and the Word was made flesh" (1:1, 14). It is usually developed in theology with much attention to the doctrinal problematic of true divinity and true humanity in the unity of the one person of Jesus Christ.

In *Redemptor Hominis,* Pope John Paul II gracefully assumes this descending pattern of christological thought. He begins with the affirmation that Jesus Christ, the Word of God, became a human being: "God entered the history of humanity and, as a human being, became an actor in that history, one of the thousands of millions of human beings but at the same time unique!" (paragraph 1). This incarnation is a radically real one. Christ who is the Son of the living God nevertheless became for our sakes a genuine human being: "He worked with human hands, he thought with a human mind. He acted with a human will, and he loved with a human heart. Born of the Virgin Mary, he has truly been made one of us, like to us in all things except sin" (8). It is this humanity of the Son of God which attracts us and which speaks even to many who are not Christian. His fidelity to the truth speaks; so does his all-embracing love and the inscrutable depth of his suffering and abandonment on the cross (7). What is to the fore, then, is Jesus Christ's personal identity. He is unmistakably God; he is also undeniably one of us.

In John Paul's hands, it is the union of the two in Jesus

Christ that triggers the drama of redemption. The whole natural world, which God created good, has lost its link with God through the sin of Adam. And the human race, specially created in the image and likeness of God, has likewise been disfigured through the sin of Adam. In the person of the new Adam, however, who joins the created with the uncreated, the world's link with God is reforged. So too the image of God in human beings is restored, for "by his Incarnation, he, the Son of God, in a certain way united himself with each human being" (8). We all, then, Jew and Greek, slave and free, male and female, indeed the whole world, are made into a new creation.

The element which John Paul sifts out of this story of redemption and begins to use to shape a vision of the church's mission in the world is the unsurpassable dignity of every human being. The descent of the eternal Word into humanity leaves no human being unaffected: "human nature, by the very fact that it was assumed, not absorbed, in him, has been raised in us also to a dignity beyond compare" (8). The result is the establishment of the unsurpassed worth of every human being. How very precious we all must be in the eyes of God that we have been given such a Redeemer, God's own Son! How very precious we are in the light of the revelation that our humanity has been restored to the likeness of God! How very precious we are, united to Christ in the mystery of redemption! What arises in us as we assimilate this christology is wonder at the goodness of God and deep amazement at ourselves. In reality, another name for this deep amazement at our worth and dignity as human beings is the gospel, the good news (10).

At this point in the development of his christology, John Paul makes the critical move which will lead to incorporating concern for social justice into the church's mission in the world. This move consists in setting up the relation between Christ and the church according to the metaphor of the *way*: "Jesus Christ is the chief way for the church. He himself is our

way . . ." (13). The church is the community of disciples, each
of whom is called in a different way to follow the one way who
is Christ (21). And where does this way lead? It leads to
human beings, to every one in the concrete and to all in our
communal and global interrelations. Out of regard for Christ,
the church must understand its own true mission as that of
being sensitive to whatever serves human well-being or threat-
ens it. Whatever else it may do, John Paul argues, the church
cannot abandon human beings for each one is unbreakably
united to Christ and enjoys a dignity that he died to restore.
Jesus Christ is the way for the church, and that way, the way of
God incarnate, leads to human beings. Thus is a dynamic link
forged between belief in the incarnate Redeemer and concern
for the public issues which affect the well-being of billions of
persons.

The logic is inexorable. If the Redeemer loves the human
race and everyone in it; if Christ took humanity to himself in
such a way as to be truly united to every person (recall the
judgment scene in Matthew 25: "as long as you did it to one
of the least of these, you did it to me"); if as a result the human
dignity of each person has been raised to a value beyond
compare, sealed with the very blood of Christ, then following
the way of its Lord the church must also have as a primary
concern the promotion of the dignity of human beings. How
could it be otherwise, if the church has entered into the
amazement of the redemptive good news? It is intrinsic to its
mission "to make human life ever more human" (14) in the
power of the name and Spirit of Christ.

Following out the logic of this approach, the door is now
opened for a host of world problems to enter and claim the
church's attention. John Paul goes on in this encyclical to
discuss the military arms race going on at the expense of the
poor of the world; nuclear weapons which make possible
such a terrible end; burgeoning technology which does not
respect human needs; the starvation of millions in the face of

the consumerism of others; the need for transformation of structures of economic life; exploitation and pollution of the planet which in the end will leave us with no home at all; torture, terrorism, violations of human rights, and discrimination of all kinds; disrespect for the unborn; imperialism and political domination. In no case is the concern of today's generation of disciples of Christ about these matters simply an adjunct to the heart of faith, or their engagement in these issues simply a practical, extrinsic application of important principles. Rather, it belongs to the essence of faith itself to care about these things—if we have been grasped by radical amazement at the good news that the human race has been redeemed by Christ and is precious to God.

Here, then, is one example of a descending christology which issues in action on behalf of justice as a constitutive element of faith itself. It begins in heaven, traces the descent of the eternal Son of God into the world, realizes the redemptive effect this has had on the dignity of each person and on all of the human race together, and then follows the Redeemer along the way of cruciform love in working out the fulfillment of this redemption in the concrete circumstances of our communal life. As John Paul II eloquently put it,

> The redemption of the world—this tremendous mystery of love in which creation is renewed—is at its deepest root the fullness of justice in a human heart, the heart of the first-born Son, in order that it may become justice in the hearts of many human beings . . called to grace, called to love. (9)

Ascending Christology

This type of christology, actually the earliest to develop, has recently been rediscovered in the church thanks to biblical scholars and their critical wizardry with scriptural texts. It begins its thinking on earth, with the memory of Jesus of

Nazareth who lived a genuinely free, historical life. It tells the story of his compassionate ministry and of his impact on the women and men who followed him. As its name suggests, this christology then traces the ascent of Jesus to the One he called *Abba,* fascinated with the dialectical mystery of death and resurrection—ugly, abandoned, human death and God's sheer gift of new, transformed life. The one who had shared our lot in all things, had announced the nearness of the reign of God, who had taken the part of the marginalized, and who had been broken in being made sin for us, is now forever with God in glory. Thus the risen Christ in person is the beginning of the new creation. As crucified Lord of history, he reveals the compassion and victory of God and, through the power of his Spirit, continues to free human beings from bondage to the powers of this age, chief among them sin and death. Indeed, in Christ the promised redemption has already begun, although its fulfillment awaits a future day. Thus, the genuine ascent of the ministering-crucified-risen Jesus into the life of God is a redemptive event par excellence. Jesus Christ's historical life which issued in our redemption is the abiding basis and necessary criterion for all proclamations of his ultimate identity. This pattern of christology finds its scriptural paradigm in the synoptic gospels of Mark, Matthew, and Luke. It is usually developed in theology with much attention to the historical circumstances of the ministry and destiny of Jesus, to his relation with his *Abba* revealed therein, and to the presence of his Spirit in the world.

In their pastoral letters on peace and on economic justice, the Catholic bishops of the United States make attractive use of this ascending pattern of christology in working out a theology of social justice. They begin in each case by remembering telling characteristics of the historical person and ministry of Jesus. The story they tell is a short one, a beautiful one, a poignant one, but it evokes a memory powerful enough to challenge us to discipleship. At the center of this story is the

symbol of the reign of God. This extraordinary biblical symbol evokes the final age when the Spirit will be poured out,
when creation will be made whole, when the Spirit-filled
servant of God will appear to bring forth justice to the na-
tions, when justice will dwell in the land, when there will be
no more war, when the lion will lie down with the lamb,
when justice and peace shall kiss—in other words, when
God's will is finally done on earth as it is in heaven and the
well-being and salvation of every human person and of all
creation is secured.

The story of Jesus is situated within the context of the
Jewish tradition's tenacious hope for the coming of this reign
of God. His prophetic ministry began with an announcement
of the good news that it was near: "The reign of God is at
hand; repent and believe in the gospel" (Mk 1:15). In this new
reality, as Jesus saw it, the longings of the "little ones" of the
world are especially fulfilled: the poor are included; mourners
are comforted; those who hunger and thirst for justice are
satisfied; the merciful, the pure of heart, those who have been
persecuted are blessed of God, the peacemakers are called
children of God (Mt 5:3–10). Little wonder that joy and
feasting accompanied Jesus' announcement that the reign of
God was near. This proclamation was coupled with a call to
conversion, to turning from the ways of violence and self-
ishness in one's own life. Giving oneself over to the reign of
God involved persons in a new way of life together, a way
marked by mercy and justice, and by love as an active, life-
giving, peacemaking force.

The story picks up tempo as the bishops remember that
Jesus' words did not remain an abstract ideal, but in his own
behavior he powerfully enacted the values of the reign of God.
He welcomed all who came to him, excluding no one on the
basis of their status or previous behavior. He healed people's
bodies and spirits, releasing them from the demons which
possessed them and returning them to life in community. He

forgave sins, restoring people to peace with themselves, with one another and with God. He pointed out the injustices of his time and opposed those who laid heavy burdens upon the people. Nor was this activity an expression of superficial niceness, for he acted aggressively and dramatically at times, such as when he cleansed the temple. "In doing these things," according to the bishops' interpretation, "he made the tender mercy of God present in a world which knew violence, oppression and injustice" (*The Challenge of Peace,* 48). Jesus himself was the person in whom the reign of God was dawning.

The bishops are very clear about the fact that in the light of the ministry just narrated, the death of Jesus historically was no accident. His preaching and enacting of the coming reign of God posed a threat to the established givens of religious and civil power. In love and fidelity to the compassionate will of his *Abba,* Jesus would not desist. The price he paid was his life: "Jesus' message and his actions were dangerous ones in his time, and they led to his death—a cruel and viciously inflicted death, a criminal's death (Gal 3:13)" (*The Challenge of Peace,* 49). He lived out fidelity to the reign of God to the end, forgiving even those who were killing him.

The story does not end here. As Jesus had proclaimed, the loving power of God is stronger even than death. God raised the crucified Jesus to life. The resurrection is the strongest possible sign that God really can be trusted to have the last word, which is life. Now, in the crucified and risen Jesus Christ, the arrival of the reign of God, the fullness of salvation, the reconciliation between God and the world finally become fully possible. In the light of this event the bishops confess the Christian belief that Jesus is the long-awaited Messiah, the Christ, in whose coming the reign of God has also begun to arrive.

At this point in the story, the bishops make a move crucial for understanding the mission of the church to be inclusive of the concerns of social justice. They characterize the church as the community of believers, founded on the call to follow Jesus, which means imitating the pattern of his life, continuing the proclamation and enactment of the reign of God. As with John Paul II but in a different context, the operative category for the identity of the Church is that of discipleship, or following the way of Jesus. In the light of the telling of the story of Jesus, this becomes a very concrete way. To be a disciple means to put one's feet in the footsteps of Jesus and, in the power of his Spirit, to continue in one's own historical time and place his mission of announcing and signing the coming of the reign of God. Together as church, the community of disciples is in a unique way called to be the instrument of the reign of God in history. Since peace and justice are among the most powerful signs of the reign of God present in this world, it belongs to the essential mission of the church to make these realities more visible in our time, so marked by oppression, violence, injustice, and threat of total destruction. Following Jesus on this way may well cost disciples their lives—the servants are not greater than the master. But the community of disciples must go on witnessing throughout the conflicts of history, drawing courage from their memory of Jesus, from their experience of his continuing presence in the Spirit, and from hope in the final victory of the coming reign of God.

Drawing out the inexorable logic of their christological position, the bishops in the end declare their specific teaching:

> Peacemaking is not an optional commitment. It is a requirement of our faith. We are called to be peacemakers not by some movement of the moment, but by our Lord Jesus. The content and context of our peacemaking is set not by some political agenda or ideological program, but by the teaching of his Church (*The Challenge of Peace,* 333).

And again:

> The concerns [of economic justice for all] are not all peripheral to the central mystery at the heart of the church. They

are integral to the proclamation of the Gospel and part of the vocation of every Christian today (*Economic Justice for All*, 60).

If we as church are truly following our risen Lord, making his historical concerns our own and committing our lives to the coming victory of the reign of God, then we are compelled to be involved in critical peacemaking and economic issues where the *shalom* and well-being of all peoples, and indeed of the whole earth, are at stake.

Here, then, are examples of a christology from below which issue in the realization that action on behalf of justice is a constitutive dimension of faith. It begins its thinking on earth with the gospel memory of the life of Jesus, and finds there the basis for the discernment of how the risen Christ is operative in the world today. The paradigmatic role of Jesus on earth becomes a source of light and energy fueling the church's own mission in the world.

Outcome: Justice

Tracing these two basically different patterns of christological thought brings us to the same point of intrinsic concern for social justice on this earth. In descending christology, the focus is on the redemptive incarnation of the eternal Word of God. So pure is this type of christology in the thinking of John Paul II that in crafting his argument he never appeals to the ministry of Jesus, making only once a passing reference to that ministry in suggesting that the parable of the last judgment in Matthew 25 might serve as an outline for an examination of conscience (16). Reflecting on this descending pattern of thought, we are invited to ponder the identification of the incarnate Word with the humanity of every person, gifting each of us with an extraordinary dignity.

In ascending christology, the focus is on the risen Jesus

Christ who was crucified as a result of a very particular kind of ministry. So clear is this type of christology in the bishops' peace pastoral that in crafting their argument they never appeal to the doctrine of the incarnation, mentioning only once, in the last paragraph, Jesus Christ under the aspect of the Word incarnate (339); in the economic justice pastoral no such reference is made at all. Reflecting on this pattern of thought we are invited to enter into the joyful, conflictual story of Jesus' ministry of justice and peace, culminating in his death and resurrection, a process which empowers us to proclaim and enact the coming of the reign of God in our own age.

While descending christology is more philosophical in character and ascending christology more historically oriented, not only are they not mutually exclusive, but both are needed for the fullness of the church's faith confession. In both, however, the bottom line is the insight that the church is gifted with the Spirit of Christ and called to discipleship with a mission patterned on the way of Jesus Christ. Whether reflection about him proceeds from above or from below, what is not possible for believers in the end is indifference to the systemic forces in the world which create so much terror and misery. In both types of christology, the final moral imperative is the same: action on behalf of justice and participation in the transformation of the world are constitutive dimensions of the church's mission for the redemption of the human race (1971 Synod of Bishops, *Justice in the World*, 6).

It seems that the church in our time is crossing the Rubicon from a land of privatized piety accompanied by deeds of charity to individuals, at times outstandingly splendid deeds, to a frontier imbued with a spirituality of justice. In this new envisionment of discipleship, individual persons are certainly not neglected but cared for within the larger structured complexities of an interdependent, suffering world. Under the impulse of a spirituality of justice, we are realizing in a new way that the gracious power of the incarnate Word and risen Christ cannot be limited to the personal and interpersonal realms alone, but includes the body politic, the social systems which we create and which in turn shape us. We are seeing anew the working of the demonic in this world, and hearing the call to enter into the way of suffering love in order to disrupt the demonic and make room for the new creation to bud forth. We are learning to love this world deeply and at the same time to be profoundly critical of its self-destructive and unjust tendencies. We are finding that in the struggle for justice and peace the moral and the religious converge, and experiencing that in this struggle our union with God is constituted. If studies are correct which show that many Catholics in the United States are resisting the leadership of the pope and bishops in this direction, it may well be that the christological emphasis in preaching, religious education, and adult formation programs needs to be revitalized so that the intrinsic and dynamic link between christology and social justice can emerge and grasp the hearts of believers.

Readings

The encyclical *Redemptor Hominis* by John Paul II is officially translated as *Redeemer of Man* (Washington, DC: U.S. Catholic Conference, 1979). The pastoral letters of the United States Catholic Bishops are *The Challenge of Peace: God's Promise and Our Response* (Washington, DC: U.S. Catholic Conference, 1983), and *Economic Justice for All: Catholic Social Teaching and the U.S. Economy* (Washington, DC: U.S. Catholic Conference, 1986). Commentary and critical analysis of the peace pastoral is carried forward in Philip Murnion, ed., *Catholics and Nuclear War* (New York: Crossroad, 1983); and Judith Dwyer, ed., *The Catholic Bishops and Nuclear War* (Washington, DC: Georgetown University Press, 1984). Reflections on the economic pastoral are found in

Thomas Gannon, ed., *The Catholic Challenge to the American Economy* (New York: Macmillan, 1987).

Renewing the Earth: Catholic Documents on Peace, Justice and Liberation, David O'Brien and Thomas Shannon, eds. (Garden City, NY: Doubleday, 1977), compiles earlier social teaching by the popes and bishops' conferences of North and Latin America. Influential theological essays which explore the background of that teaching have been gathered in *Official Catholic Social Teaching,* Charles Curran and Richard McCormick, eds. (New York: Paulist, 1986). David Hollenbach has written an excellent analysis in *Justice, Peace and Human Rights* (New York: Crossroad, 1988).

The theological links between christology and social justice are worked out in powerful and readable fashion in *Above Every Name: The Lordship of Christ and Social Systems,* Thomas Clarke, ed. (New York: Paulist, 1980). Sharon Ringe, *Jesus, Liberation and the Biblical Jubilee* (Philadelphia: Fortress, 1985), presents biblical images which link ethics and christology. The fundamental moves involved are explored by Joe Holland and Peter Henriot, *Social Analysis: Linking Faith and Justice* (Maryknoll, NY: Orbis, 1984). Carol Frances Jegen, *Jesus the Peacemaker* (Kansas City, MO: Sheed and Ward, 1986) is a highly readable presentation of this theme.

Kathleen and James McGinnis, *Parenting for Peace and Justice* (Maryknoll, NY: Orbis, 1981), offer practical ways for the church's social teaching to influence the younger generation. Karl Rahner's view of the descending and ascending types of christology is described in "Two Basic Types of Christology," *Theological Investigations* 13 (New York: Seabury, 1975), 213–23.

6

Liberation Christology

The realization that concern for justice is an intrinsic part of christology receives a sharper and more critical focus when it is articulated by people who are actually suffering from injustice. The major Catholic theologians who developed transcendental christology in the 1960's, recovering the genuine humanity of Jesus, and narrative christology in the 1970's, recovering the history of Jesus, have a great deal in common: they are all white, well-fed, well-educated, prosperous, privileged, European males. They all theologize, however compassionately, out of an experience of political, economic, and social privilege. Starting in the 1970's and moving into the 1980's, a third wave of renewal in Catholic christology has developed as the poor and dispossessed in the world have begun to find their voice. On virtually every continent, reflection on faith from the "underside of history" has resulted in forms of theology collectively known as liberation theology. It is a new way of doing theology, one which draws on the experience of systematically oppressed and suffering peoples. Done from a different perspective, it has different characteristics and method from either the transcendental or narrative approach.

Liberation theology originated in Latin America after the Second Vatican Council, although its roots reach back into the base-community movement begun decades earlier. Theologians such as Leonardo Boff, Jon Sobrino, and Juan Luis Segundo have used its methods to present a new answer to the christological question, one which sees Jesus Christ as the Liberator. Such theology is not limited to one continent, however. With differences according to the circumstances of oppression, similar work is being done in Africa (e.g., Albert Nolan), the Asian subcontinent (e.g., Aloysius Pieris), Indonesia, and the Philippines. It poses a profound challenge to the conscience of disciples who live relatively safe and prosperous lives in the so-called First World.

Characteristics

1. The context of liberation theology is the recognition of the suffering of a particular oppressed group. Every word here is important. While frequently interwined, oppressions differ—poverty, political disenfranchisement, patriarchy, apartheid, etc.—so that not all liberation theology is the same. Again, individuals suffer, but liberation theology is generated when community is formed. Coming together in faith, people become conscious of their situation, pray, study the scriptures, and seek actions which will begin to change things for the better. Out of this interaction, reflections on the meaning of faith arise. As part of these groups, theologians are able to articulate these insights systematically, but it is basically a people's theology coming from the grass roots.

Recognition of the oppression and suffering which have so many in their grip gives rise to a sense of outrage. One cries out: This should not be. The bishops of Latin America, for example, at the Medellin conference in 1968 wrote in the opening lines of their document on justice: "The misery that besets large masses of human beings in all of our countries is described in [many] studies. That misery, as a collective fact, expresses itself as injustice which cries to the heavens." The lack of food, shelter, education, and medical care, especially for untold numbers of children, contrasts with what is necessary for a decent human life and creates a climate of collective anguish which makes us genuinely scandalized. This sense of outrage is a religious experience. Impelling the judgment that the situation is against the will of the living God, it awakens a strong moral imperative in the Christian conscience to resist. Letting it go on is to have complicity in the wrongness.

The context of liberation theology, then, is different from other forms of theology. It is shaped by the experience of oppression, within groups who become conscious of this and come together to work and pray with the sense that the situation *must* change.

2. The reflection of liberation theology is intrinsically intertwined with what is called praxis, or critical action done reflectively. Juan Luis Segundo, a Latin American theologian, argues that as a process of thinking, liberation theology is an owl—it arises at sundown after a full day of activity. In other words, when people who are engaged in action on behalf of justice come together to pray and talk about their situation and reflect on God in relation to what is going on, what emerges is liberation theology. Thought and action mutually feed each other. A very practical engagement with forces of oppression, therefore, is intrinsic to the doing of liberation theology. In fact, a convincing case can be made that if one is not engaged in action on behalf of justice, then one simply cannot do liberation theology. One of the key ingredients would be missing.

3. Liberation theology is highly conscious of the social nature of human existence. An essential aspect of each of us as individuals is our relatedness to one another, along with the structures we have created to embody that relatedness. There simply is no such creature as an individual person outside this network of relationships. Therefore sin, as it affects the human heart and is utterly personal, is also social and shows up in the way we structure ourselves as a community. It affects how people, over time, have distributed power, and is embodied in the present as bad decisions of the past continue to be

sedimented in structures. In addition to thinking of sin as an individual act, one must also think of it collectively, socially, in structural terms. Similarly, the grace of God forgives individual sin and unites each person with God; but it not only transforms us one by one. It is also social, embedded in structures, and able to transform them. There is a great consciousness of this sociality of human existence in liberation theology, and the perspective is far from the privatized view too often prevalent among those who are privileged.

4. Liberation theology makes extensive use of social analysis. Unlike classical and transcendental theology, whose "handmaid" was philosophy, and unlike narrative christology which makes a partner of historical and biblical studies, this approach utilizes social, political, economic, and anthropological studies which lay bare the structures of the social situation. With the help of these disciplines, the situation is analyzed to identify the forces that are causing the suffering. What are the dynamics of a system of privilege for the few which causes misery for the many? Who is benefitting from the way things are arranged? Indeed, who benefits from any particular theological interpretation? Because it asks these kinds of questions liberation theology almost invariably comes up critical of the status quo. Being done in a social situation of oppression, it names evils and perceives a way forward certain of one thing: that structures must change. From the perspective of the victims, the chasm between what should be and what actually is is so great that superficial reforms of tinkering with the system simply will not do. Liberation theology opts for the changing of structures, and that means it is a conflictual theology, for the powerful are fiercely protective of their own privilege.

5. In addition to the goal of classical theology, which was to understand the faith, the goal of liberation theology includes the purpose of changing the unjust situation. It is a practical goal in addition to an intellectual one that is endorsed. Theology here is seeking not just the gift of meaning

from newly interpreted dogmas, but also the release of captives. It intends to contribute something to the lifting of misery for actual people here and now.

6. The vision which impels liberation theology is that of the reign of God, already arriving. We do not have to wait until the last day for God to wipe all tears away from people's faces and for there to be an end to mourning. The new heaven and the new earth should already be beginning to take root, if not totally, then at least in real anticipations here and now. To use a technical word, what is operative is a realized eschatology which functions as a critique of the lack of salvation in present situations.

In this vision, what comes to the fore in a new way is the importance of this world, in contrast with a dualism which would pit heaven against earth. In a dualistic view, what happens on earth is relatively unimportant because we expect a life to come where eternal reward and punishment will be meted out. The more integrated vision proposed by Vatican II and strongly adopted by liberation theology sees that this world also matters, for it mediates to us in a sacramental way the goodness of God. Our ultimate salvation can be tasted in advance in the blessings of this world. In very concrete ways, then, God's saving will is violated when oppressive situations grind people down; but God's saving will appears wherever justice and peace gain a foothold. As the Latin American bishops said at Medellin: "All liberation is an anticipation of the complete redemption brought by Christ." This redemption involves us as persons in all of our dimensions, so that no act of lifting oppression, however small, is divorced from the final redemption. Rather, it is part of salvation already happening.

Method

Individual theologians will work variations on the theme, but liberation theology's method does involve three steps.

First, an oppressive situation is recognized to be oppressive. It is named a sin and analyzed for its root causes. Then, because this is theology and not simply a humanistic discipline, Christian tradition is analyzed for what may have contributed to this oppression. What elements coming from our tradition had a hand in this present circumstance? Where is the complicity of the church and its preaching? How have we understood Christ in a way that is helpful to the oppressor? At this point liberation theology becomes quite critical of some elements of the tradition. Finally, guided by the experience of the oppressed, the Christian tradition is searched for elements that would yield a new understanding and a new practice which would be liberating. At this point liberation theology often notices things in our tradition that have been overlooked and lifts them up as a challenge to accepted interpretations.

Jesus Christ

"Who do you say that I am?" In Latin American liberation theology the question begins to be answered by bringing into focus the poverty of millions of people. The question arises: is it God's will that these people be deprived of livelihood, that they be malnourished, that children die, that there be inadequate education, no medical benefits, no shelter for millions of people? Is this what God desires? No, it is wrong. Then why is it like this? At this point social analysis starts to uncover economic and political structures wherein the majority of people are landless while a small minority of people own all the land. The land itself is worked by the many for the benefit of the few. This in itself is a controversial analysis. The dispute over its legitimacy brings to mind Brazilian Bishop Dom Helder Camara's comment: "When I ask people for bread to feed the poor, they think I am a saint; when I ask them *why* the poor are hungry, they think I am a Communist." But it is that asking of the question *why* that gets to the root causes.

Then it becomes possible to envision something besides just emergency measures and endless patching up; a radical, creative quest for better structures ensues.

The second step toward answering the question leads to critical analysis of the way preaching and piety, with official encouragement, have appropriated the tradition about Jesus Christ. What is there in the tradition of christology that has supported this situation of injustice? Two things have been named. The first is the mysticism of the dead Christ in Latin American piety, symbolized in graphic crucifixes and in Holy Week processions in which the dead Christ is carried and pious folk mourn as if he had just died. This is coupled with an interior spiritual identification with Christ as a model. What is wrong with this? How has this contributed to the continuation of a situation of oppression? Emphasis on the dead Christ works to legitimate suffering as the will of God. It is preached that Jesus Christ suffered quietly and passively; he went to the cross like a sheep to the slaughter and opened not his mouth. The corollary is clear: To be a good Christian you should suffer quietly; you should go to the cross and not open your mouth; you should bear your cross in this world and after death God will give you your eternal reward. When embraced in a situation of injustice, this pattern of piety promotes acceptance of the status of victim. Anyone who would challenge their suffering would be seen to go against the example of Christ. This obviously works to the advantage of the oppressor.

The second difficulty that has been identified in the tradition is the glorification of the imperial Christ. In heaven the risen Christ rules. It is preached that he sets up on earth human authorities to rule in his name, both in the civil and ecclesiastical spheres. Human authorities represent Christ and are to be obeyed as one would obey him. In a situation of injustice, this puts Christ in league with the dominating powers. The ethics which flow from it would lead one to think that anyone who challenged temporal or ecclesiastical rulers, all too often allies in the past history of Latin America, was disobeying the will of God. This emphasis on the heavenly Christ ruling as Lord in league with the earthly lords has been used to keep people passive in the face of their own oppression.

The third step is then taken. What in the tradition of christology has been overlooked and, in the light of the experience of the poor, might be used to shape a christology that would liberate? Liberation theologians look primarily to the Jesus of the gospels. Is he really a passive victim whose example legitimates passive suffering? Is he really a dominating lord whose will legitimates oppressive rule? What did he stand for in his ministry? What about the fact that his ministry to the outcast and sinners led to his death in an intrinsic and profound way? Is the resurrection not God's victory over oppressive forces? Reading the scriptures from the perspective of the poor makes it very clear (and this comes as a surprise, perhaps, to those who have not been suffering, but to the oppressed it comes as a great revelation of good news) that Jesus is on the side of the downtrodden and calls oppressors to conversion. A key text is the scene in Luke where, at the beginning of his ministry, Jesus goes to his home synagogue in Nazareth and reads from the scroll of Isaiah. Imagine how these words sound to people within a situation of oppression:

> The Spirit of the Lord is upon me, because he has anointed me to preach the good news to the poor; he has sent me to proclaim release to the captives and recovering of sight to the blind, to set at liberty those who are oppressed, to proclaim the acceptable year of the Lord.

Sitting down Jesus says, "Today this scripture is being fulfilled in your hearing" (Lk 4:16–21). This prophecy sets the agenda for Jesus' ministry, as we see from everything that follows in the gospels. His preaching that the reign of God is near; his singling out the poor and those who hunger after justice for beatitude; the way he feeds and heals and welcomes out-casts—all of this reveals a choice, a preference for those who have not. Obviously, then, this is God's agenda for the poor: that they be released and set at liberty from grinding poverty and oppression. This is special good news for victims. It means that their present situation is not the last word about their lives, but that God has another design in mind. Touching structures as well as hearts, God is opening up a new future for the poor.

One of the most powerful expressions of this gospel truth is the Magnificat, the song of Mary. After praising God for all the great things He has done for her, a poor peasant woman, she goes on to sing about the great things God will do for everyone else, perceiving this in very startling words: "He has put down the mighty from their thrones and has exalted the lowly. He has filled the hungry with good things and has sent the rich way empty" (Lk 2:46–55). How does that sound to the hearts of those oppressed? There is a clear message enun-ciated here that rings all the way through the gospels: Jesus opts for the poor, for the cause of the poor, as the embodi-ment of God who does the same.

If this is the way the ministry of Jesus is read in liberation theology, then it flows logically into an interpretation of the cross as a liberating event. It is not that Jesus came to die; he was not masochistic. He came to live and to bring life abun-dantly to everyone else. Doing so faithfully, however, put him at odds with the religious and civil powers not tuned into God's ways. In one real sense the crucified Jesus is a victim arrested, unjustly tried, executed. But he is far from passive. His death results from a very active ministry in which love and compassion for the dispossessed led him into conflict with the powerful. Even in custody he still had the choice of what attitude to adopt toward those who were torturing and killing him. His words, "Father, forgive them, for they know not what

they do" (Lk 23:34) show that his choice was still for love and
compassion. There is active engagement here, of heart and
soul, in conflict with the mystery of evil and in tune with the
mystery of the goodness of God. In the end, the cross reveals
that God identifies with the one unjustly executed rather than
with the rulers. Far from legitimizing suffering, the cross in a
liberation perspective shows victims that God is in powerful
solidarity with them in their suffering, and opens the possibility of their own active engagement, both interiorly and
exteriorly, against the forces of oppression.

Coherent with this reading, the resurrection appears as the
sign of God's liberation breaking into this world. It does not
rob Jesus' death of its negative aspects, but reveals that ultimately the loving power of God is stronger than death and
evil. The risen Christ embodies God's intention on behalf of
everyone who is oppressed; in the end, the murderer will not
triumph over his victim. In this light, the ruling Christ is seen
to be in league not with dominating powers who cause so
much suffering, but with those who suffer, as ground of their
hope. He is the Lord as the crucified one who liberates.

Out of this reading of the story of Jesus from the perspective of the poor and oppressed has come a new and potent
christological title: Jesus Christ, Liberator. In the early
church, believers borrowed names which had currency in civil
society and bestowed them on Jesus, whose own life history
and Spirit filled them with a different significance. For example, the title "Lord," used of someone who was a boss or an
overseer of a group, was given to Jesus in acknowledgment of
his ascendency over all other powers of this world. The dif-
ference which his own history gave to this title was the value of
liberating service rather than domination: this Lord washes
feet. A similar dynamic occurs with this new title. Some
leaders of movements for national independence in various
countries have been called "Liberator," showing the role they
played in freeing their people from dominating colonial na-

tions. Giving this title to Jesus, liberation theology intends to confess his identification with the oppressed as well as the power of his name and Spirit to overturn that oppression. If people set their hearts on him, they will be on the path to wholeness and freedom. At the same time, Jesus' own life history breaks open the secular meaning of the title and revises it. He is Liberator not just for one group, but especially for the poor as sign of inclusion of all. Through him God's will for the justice and well-being of the whole world, through the lifting up of the lowliest, comes into play. Again, he is Liberator not in a violent or military way, but through active ministry, boldness in speaking, steadfastness in conflict, suffering love, and ultimate reliance on God.

Jesus Christ, Liberator, is a christological theme that evokes a new image of God, who is on the side of the oppressed with the aim to free them. It also lifts up a new image of the oppressed, of great worth, the privileged focus of God's own care. Finally, it gives us a new image of discipleship, entering into the way of Jesus with the poor, a way which has a paschal character. It carries a new answer to the question, "Who do you say I am?" Neither passive victim nor dominating Lord, Jesus is the liberating Word of God in solidarity with the poor.

As christology, the liberation approach is more practical than theoretical in its intent. In classical terms, it is more functional than ontological, focusing more on the saving, liberating power of Jesus Christ than on his inner makeup. Such a christology calls the church to discipleship, to participation with God in the work of overturning oppression. In order for Christians who are not involved directly with a particular situation of oppression to hear this call, what is needed is conversion. The cry of the poor must be heeded and their perspective entered into. Ultimately, however, liberation theology has made it plain that none of us is uninvolved, like it or not. The network of oppressive structures is an interlinked reality around the world, with local manifestations. Not to acknowledge this is to remain in complicity with these forces. We have lost our innocence on this question—neutrality is not possible. We may ignore the situation and implicitly opt for the status quo with its damaging effect on millions of people. Or we can name Jesus Christ "Liberator," thereby committing ourselves personally and ecclesially to enter with Christ into the struggle for justice.

Readings

Major Catholic Latin American christologies which are available in English are: Leonardo Boff, *Jesus Christ Liberator* (Maryknoll, NY: Orbis, 1978); Jon Sobrino, *Christology at the Crossroads* (Maryknoll, NY: Orbis, 1978), as well as his collected essays *Jesus in Latin America* (Maryknoll, NY: Orbis, 1987); and the five-volume work by Juan Luis Segundo collectively entitled *Jesus of Nazareth Yesterday and Today,* especially vol. 2, *The Historical Jesus of the Synoptics* (Maryknoll, NY: Orbis, 1985), and vol. 3 *The Humanist Christology of Paul* (Maryknoll, NY: Orbis, 1986). José Miguez-Bonino, ed., *Faces of Jesus: Latin American Christologies* (Maryknoll, NY: Orbis, 1984), provides an excellent sampler of liberation christology.

For most North American readers, liberation theology needs to be mediated since the circumstances of the two continents differ so profoundly. Very fine interpretations are offered by Roger Haight, *An Alternative Vision* (New York: Paulist, 1985); Rebecca Chopp, *The Praxis of Suffering* (Maryknoll, NY: Orbis, 1986); Philip Berryman, *Liberation Theology* (Bloomington, IN: Meyer-Stone Books, 1987); and Michael Cook, "Jesus from the Other Side of History: Christology in Latin America," *Theological Studies* 44 (1983) 258–87.

Liberation theology is not confined to Latin America, however. For statements of this basic intuition from other contexts, see James Cone, *A Black Theology of Liberation* (Philadelphia: Lippincott, 1970); Vine Deloria, *God Is Red* (New York: Grosset and Dunlap,

1973); Virgilio Elizondo, *Galilean Journey: The Mexican American Promise* (Maryknoll, NY: Orbis, 1983); Albert Nolan, *Jesus Before Christianity* (Maryknoll, NY: Orbis, 1970), which focuses on South Africa; and Aloysius Pieris, *An Asian Theology of Liberation* (Maryknoll, NY: Orbis, 1988).

7

Feminist Christology

Almost all theology in the Christian tradition, including liberation theology done from the perspective of the poor and oppressed, has been done by male theologians. In our day we are witnessing the phenomenon that all over the world the "other half" of the human race, women, are waking up to their own dignity and finding their own voice. One result has been that within the community of disciples, faith is now being reflected upon explicitly from the perspective and experience of women. This type of theology is commonly called feminist theology, or theology based upon the conviction that women share equally with men in the dignity of being human. The christological question "Who do you say that I am?" receives a response with yet another dimension when answered from the experience of believing women.

Types

There are many types of feminist theology, but they can be divided roughly into two categories. One is called revolutionary feminist theology and the other reformist. The revolutionary school of thought is produced by women who, upon examining the Christian tradition, find it so male-dominated that they pronounce it hopelessly irredeemable. These women have usually voted with their feet and have left the church, a growing phenomenon at least in some countries. Purging religion of its male-dominating elements, they form groups to pray and worship together in which sisterhood is the great value and the deity addressed is the goddess. Obviously, revolutionary feminist theologians would not be interested in typical Catholic theology, let alone reflection on Jesus Christ. On the other hand, while agreeing about the male-dominated character of the Christian tradition, reformist feminist theologians find reason to hope that it may be transformed, for this tradition also contains powerful liberating elements. Thus they choose to stay within the church and work for reform. Within this group there are many different approaches (fundamentalist, symbolic, liberal) but interestingly, the majority of Catholic feminist theologians such as Rosemary Radford Ruether, Elisabeth Schüssler Fiorenza, Anne Carr, and Margaret Farley work with the liberation model in the sense that they seek the dismantling of patriarchy and equal justice especially for the dispossessed. This is the perspective that will be explored here.

Characteristics

The same characteristics that mark liberation theology as a whole also mark feminist liberation theology. It arises out of the recognition of the suffering of a particular oppressed group, in this case women. Consciousness of the ways women are perpetually relegated to second-class citizenship in society and church, in contrast to women's essential human dignity, gives rise to outrage: this should not be; this is against the will of God. Reflection arises in groups actively engaged in praxis, or prayerful resistance to patriarchal oppression. Sedimented in structures, the social nature of the sin of sexism is laid bare by feminist social analysis. The goal of this form of theologizing is not only to understand the meaning of the faith tradition, but also to change it insofar as it has not meant good news for human beings who are women. Finally, the vision which guides feminist theology is that of a new human community based on the values of mutuality and reciprocity. The goal is not reverse discrimination, with women dominating men; that would be the same problem in reverse. Rather, the dream of a new heaven and a new earth takes hold here, with no one group dominating and no one group being subordinated, but each person in his or her own right participating according to their gifts, without preconceived stereotyping, in genuine mutuality. It is not envisioned that everyone be the same, but that the uniqueness of each be equally respected in a community of brothers and sisters. The three steps of the method of liberation theology—analyzing the situation, searching the tradition for what contributes to the oppression, and searching again for what liberates—yield a new appreciation of the meaning of Jesus Christ for human beings who are women.

Analysis

The fundamental analysis of the situation made by feminist theologians is that sexism is pervasive. A sign of broken mutuality between the two genders, sexism like racism classifies human beings, prescribes certain roles and denies certain rights to them on the basis of physical characteristics. Just as racism assigns an inferior dignity to people on the basis of the color of their skin or ethnic heritage and labors mightily to keep people of color in their preordained "place," so too on the basis of gender sexism considers women essentially less worthy as human beings than men and sets up powerful forces to keep women in their proper "place." In both "isms," physical characteristics are made to count for the essence of the human being, so that the fundamental human dignity of the person is violated. This is to be noted: there is a fundamental interlocking of oppressions. The kind of attitude that

considers women less than genuinely human in their own
right is the same attitude which demeans people of different
race or economic class. The prejudicial attitude stems from an
inability to deal with the otherness of people who are different
from oneself or to count them as fully human as oneself.

Sexism shows itself in two ways. The first is in structures
which are so shaped that power is always in the hands of the
dominant male; other males are ranked in a series of graded
subordinations, with the least powerful forming a large base.
This kind of structure is known as patriarchy, from the Latin
pater understood as father of the family. It is best imaged as a
triangle, with control at the top and less-to-no power below.
Where do women fit into this picture? In their own right, they
do not fit in at all. In patriarchal structures, women are
defined by the men to whom they belong, with the wife of the
chief having a greater status than the women of the men at the
base. It needs little reflection to see that structures of family
life, of social, political, and economic life, and of ecclesial life,
are predominately patriarchal.

Sexism shows itself, secondly, in patterns of thinking that
take the humanity of male human beings and make it normative for all. This way of thinking is called androcentrism,
from the Greek *andros,* or adult male; its vision of humanity
is centered on the adult male. Women are considered human
not in their own right, but in a secondary way, in a way
derivative from and dependent on the male. Rather than both
genders being seen as two coequal ways in which human
nature is embodied, the male way of being in the world is
privileged as "normal," while what is unique to women is
human "by exception" to that norm.

As with patriarchal structures, it is quickly obvious that
androcentric thinking is pervasive throughout society and
church. Virtually all of the influential male theologians in the
tradition have thought in this pattern. Tertullian, for example,

is famous (or infamous) for his view of woman as the temptress, writing:

[handwritten: "1st sin, guilt, then Adam"]

[handwritten margin note: Tertullian]

[handwritten arrow and symbol]

> Do you not realize that you are each an Eve? The curse of God
> on this sex of yours lives on even in our times. Guilty, you must
> bear its hardship. You are the devil's gateway; you desecrated
> the fatal tree; you first betrayed the law of God; you softened
> up with your cajoling words the one against whom the devil
> could not prevail by force. All too easily you destroyed the
> image of God, Adam. You are the one who deserved death,
> and yet it was the Son of God who had to die.

[handwritten: He blames women for Jesus death !!]

There are dozens of statements in Augustine's writings that
make androcentrism out to be the very nature of things:

> Woman does not possess the image of God in herself, but only
> when taken together with the male who is her head, so that
> the whole substance is one image. But when she is assigned
> the role as helpmate, a function that pertains to her alone, then
> she is not the image of God. But as far as the man is concerned,
> he is by himself alone the image of God just as fully and
> completely as when he and the woman are joined together
> into one.

Following Aristotle's biology, Thomas Aquinas was of the
opinion that "woman is a misbegotten man," a physiological
view which then determined his assessment of woman's essential nature. These are but samplings of a view that is pervasive
in the Catholic tradition, influencing not only theology but
canon law and practice as well. Note that this way of thinking
about women is the product of male reflection. Left to their
own devices, women would not define themselves this way.

In sexism with its patriarchal structures and androcentric
thinking, women experience systematic oppression. They are
excluded, marginalized, and rendered invisible in language

and public life. They are subordinated in theory and practice
to men (making the tea, while men make the important
decisions). Stereotyped as mindless, emotional, weak, they are
prevented from assuming leadership roles. Women are denied
economic, legal, and educational rights, paid less money for
the same work, and in many a place made to need the sig-
nature of a man for certain transactions such as buying land.
As U.N. statistics show, while forming one-half of the world's
population, women do three-fourths of the world's work,
receive one-tenth of the world's salary, and own one one-
hundredth of the world's land. Two-thirds of illiterate adults
are women. Over three-fourths of starving people are women
and their dependent children. To make a dark picture even
bleaker, women are bodily and sexually exploited, used, bat-
tered, and raped. The fact is, men do this to women in a way
that women do not do to men. Sexism is pervasive on a global
scale.

Within these kinds of experiences, women's own self-image
comes in for a great battering. There is widespread lack of self-
esteem and self-confidence that has been documented even
among very competent women. The entire system tells women
every day that they are not quite as good as men are. In the
classical tradition, Augustine and many others are of the
opinion that pride was the original sin which caused the Fall.
Feminist theologians are of the opinion that this may well be
true for men, but that for women the original sin is more
likely the opposite: loss of a center, diffuseness of personality,
lack of a sense of self leading one to drift or take direction
unthinkingly from others. On the other hand, the system of
sexism is also demeaning to men, who are conditioned to
develop only a narrow band of human characteristics (to be
strong, rational, in control). Men are not allowed to develop
their humanity in all of its dimensions either; we all are preset
in stereotyped ways. Thus, the overcoming of sexism in a new
kind of community where women recover their full humanity

is envisioned as being very much to the advantage of the full humanity of men as well.

Out of the system of sexism in all of its manifestations, feminist theology has developed a criterion or critical principle for judging structures and theories. Phrased by Rosemary Radford Ruether, the principle is the value of the full humanity of women. Whatever enables this to flourish is redemptive and of God; whatever damages this is nonredemptive and contrary to God's intent. With this in mind, sexism itself is judged to be sinful. When Catholic theologians say this, they appeal to the Second Vatican Council. *The Church in the Modern World* (*Gaudium et Spes*, 29), in the section on human community, states: L▷ yay Shannon!

> True, all persons are not alike from the point of view of varying physical power and the diversity of intellectual and moral resources. Nevertheless, with respect to the fundamental rights of the person, every type of discrimination, whether social or cultural, whether based on sex, race, color, social condition, language or religion is to be overcome and irradicated as contrary to God's intent.

Notice that sex leads the list of the different bases of discrimination. The council goes on to give an example:

> For in truth it must still be regretted that fundamental personal rights are not universally honored. Such is the case of a woman who is denied the right and freedom to choose a husband, to embrace a state of life, or to acquire an education or cultural benefits equal to those recognized for men.

The one example used to illustrate all of these discriminations is the denial of the rights of women as persons. What is called for is transformation of the self and of social systems that support exploitative relations, the relations between men and women key among them.

1976 - Vatican No women priest

Vatican Council 62-65

What about women to priesthood?!?
- divide between teaching and Church doctrine.

Critique of Christology

The second step involves analysis of tradition and there,
when the turn is made to christology, the judgment is made
that of all the doctrines of the church christology is the one
most used to oppress women. In what way? Basically it comes
down to the way in which the maleness of Jesus has been
interpreted. That Jesus was a male human being is beyond
question. This is part of his historical particularity and is to be
respected, along with the fact that he was a carpenter who
lived in the first century, spoke Aramaic, and so on. Each of us
as a human being is characterized in such particular ways. The
problem arises when Jesus' maleness, this particular aspect of
himself as a person, is lifted up and made into a universal
principle. This then operates in two ways which contribute to
the subordination of women.

First, it comes to be taken for granted that the maleness of
Jesus reveals the maleness of God, or that the only proper way
to represent God is in male images. Certainly Jesus called
God *Abba;* and he is also presented in the gospels saying such
things as, "he who sees me sees the Father" (Jn 14:9). But due
to a literal and naive idea of revelation, this is interpreted as
meaning that God should be imaged exclusively as male, or at
least that God is more suitably thought of in analogy with
male human beings than with female. While God is Spirit,
neither male nor female but Creator of both in the divine
image, in the tradition the maleness of Jesus has been taken as
a pointer to the exclusive maleness of God. Consequently, we
have named the highest power of the universe (Ultimate Reality) in male terms, a naming which rebounds to the benefit of
male human beings. Women never find themselves charac-
terised equally in the image of God or as close to the divine. In
Genesis chapter 1, when God creates the human couple, male
and female, in the divine image, no such discrimination is
made; neither male nor female is more in the divine image

is it sexist — No both brought up in Gods image

than the other. In fact, both taken together are in the divine image. Feminist theology reasons that since both male and female are created in God's image, then presumably God can be imaged either as male or as female, always aware of the limitation of our metaphors.

In fact, in the Jewish scriptures, God is imaged in female form by some of the prophets in very moving and beautiful ways—as mother, as midwife, as nurse, as a mother bird spreading her wings over her chicks, as Sophia (Wisdom). Jesus, too, spun out female images in his preaching. The reign of God is like the yeast that a woman kneads into dough so that the whole loaf rises: this is an image of God as baker woman, kneading the yeast of the new creation into the world and working over it until the whole world rises. What a great image for God's redeeming work! Even more startling, perhaps, is the parable of the woman searching for her lost coin. This parable appears together with the parable of the good shepherd in Luke chapter 15 (1–10). They both tell the same story of God's active search for the sinner. In one, a man loses a sheep and leaves his ninety-nine others to seek for it vigorously; when he finds it, he calls upon his neighbors to rejoice. This marvelous image of God the Redeemer has worked its way into the Christian imagination. But the same drama is played out in the other story. A woman loses one of her ten coins and drops everything to search the whole house until she finds it; when she does, she calls her friends and neighbors to rejoice with her. Here we have another image of God the Redeemer. Jesus is saying that we are as precious to God, even when we sin, as money is to a woman who cares very much for it. God goes after us in the same way. The same message is being proclaimed in both stories, one in terms of male work and the other in terms of female work. Both reflect the active, consuming love of God the Redeemer. (Someday, somewhere, some bishop is going to consecrate a church to God the good homemaker; and some artist is going to draw,

paint, or sculpt God the searching woman in a way parallel to
our pictures and churches dedicated to the Good Shepherd.
Both symbols are in our tradition, but the imagination of
Christians has latched onto one and neglected the other). In a
saying reminiscent of Lady Wisdom, Jesus even referred to
himself in female imagery, wishing he could gather the people
of Jerusalem within his arms as a mother hen gathers chicks
under her wings (Mt 23:37–39).

At various times in the Christian tradition, female metaphors for God did come into use. The Syriac liturgy, for
example, refers to the Holy Spirit as our Mother. The medieval mystic Julian of Norwich understands Jesus as our
mother, nourishing us from his own body. In our own day,
Pope John Paul I said memorably that just as God is truly our
Father, even more is God our Mother, especially when we are
in trouble through sin. Overall, however, we have neglected
these scriptural and traditional images of God, seldom if ever
using them in liturgy, catechisis, or personal prayer. Instead,
we use the maleness of Jesus to concentrate on a male God.

Our language about God, furthermore, makes constant use
of the male pronoun "he," which again summons up in the
mind a male image. Even sophisticated theologians fall into
this trap, claiming, for example, "God is not male, He is
spirit." Why does it always have to be "he"? It is because we
are operating within an androcentric framework, supported
by the maleness of Jesus, which presumes that God always has
to be considered male. On the other hand, French theologian
Yves Congar has recently written a three-volume work on the
Holy Spirit in which he tries to recover the Holy Spirit as the
feminine person of God or the feminine dimension of God,
using all the scriptural images of the Spirit *(ruah)* as feminine—hovering, creating, renewing the earth. God as Spirit
may also be referred to as "she." This kind of thinking
basically breaks open the male metaphor of "father" and
makes us realize deeply the mystery of God who goes beyond

all our images and concepts. God can also be imaged in nonpersonal terms, such as rock, water, fire, and wind; the scriptures have a great deal of this. The important theological question is: Who is God and how do we best image God? But the point that feminist theologians make is that in the Christian tradition and continuing today in our ecclesial life, God is constantly referred to in male terms. The naive use of the historical maleness of Jesus is a main contributing factor.

The second way in which the maleness of Jesus has operated to subordinate women concerns human beings more than God. The gender of Jesus has been taken to be the mode or paradigm of what it means to be human. This is interpreted literally to mean that maleness is closer to the human ideal than is femaleness. Proof of this attitude is seen in reactions to a hypothetical question about the incarnation. The Word became flesh: God who is beyond gender became a human being. Could God have become a human being as a woman? The question strikes some people as silly or worse. Theologically, though, the answer is Yes. Why not? If women are genuinely human and if God is the deep mystery of holy love, then what is to prevent such an incarnation? But taking for granted the implicit inferiority of women, Christian theology has dignified maleness as the only genuine way of being human, thus making Jesus' embodiment as male an ontological necessity rather than a historical option. Owing to the way christology has been handled in an unthinking androcentric perspective, Jesus' maleness has been so interpreted that he has become the male revealer of a male God whose full representative can only be male. As a package, this christology relegates women to the margins of significance.

Feminist Liberation Christology

In searching the tradition for elements of a christology that would liberate women, feminist theologians strike gold in

Jesus' ministry, death, and resurrection, and the tradition of wisdom christology.

1. Jesus' preaching proclaims justice and peace for all people, inclusive of women. The reign of God is diametrically opposed to any group setting itself up as exclusively privileged and relegating others to the periphery. The vision of the reign of God is precisely a vision of community where every human person is valued and all interrelate in a mutually respectful way. Feminist theologians note that in Jesus' preaching it is precisely those on the periphery of established structures who are counted first in the reign of God, not in order to reverse discrimination but to break the old pattern of discrimination and set up a new pattern of relating. It sounds startling, but the prostitute will enter the kingdom of heaven before the Pharisees. Tables are turned as the sacred male religious leaders receive no priority over a woman who engages in prostitution, but the opposite happens. Jesus' preaching of the reign of God is a powerful liberating force.

2. Jesus' naming God *Abba* is also liberating, because in Jesus' understanding, *Abba* is the very opposite of a dominating patriarch. Rather, this compassionate, intimate, and close *Abba* releases everyone from patterns of domination and calls for another kind of community:

> Call no man on earth Father, for one is your Abba who is in heaven; nor should you be called leader, for only the Messiah is that. The greatest among you must be the servant. Whoever makes himself great will be humbled, and whoever humbles himself will be made great. (Mt 23:9–12)

The one *Abba* creates a human community of mutuality. Far from legitimating patriarchy, the one *Abba* subverts it, setting up in its place a community of brothers and sisters.

3. Jesus' characteristic behavior of partiality for the marginalized included women at every turn as the oppressed of the oppressed in every group. Treating women with a grace and

respect commensurate with their human dignity, Jesus healed, exorcised, forgave, and restored women to *shalom*. His table community was inclusive, and women, both sinners and those who were part of "his own" as Luke called the band of followers, shared in the joy of the approach of the reign of God. His own example has led one feminist theologian to remark that the problem is not that Jesus is a male, but that more males are not like Jesus.

4. Feminist interpretation of the stories of women in the gospels is making clear that while this point has been suppressed in our androcentric tradition, Jesus called women to be disciples. They formed part of his company in Galilee, leaving their families and homes to follow him. The wealthy among them bankrolled the ministry, providing for the needs of the community out of their own pocket (Lk 8:1–3). The names of these women are given several times in the gospels but have become a forgotten part of the story. Mary Magdalene, the "apostle to the apostles" as Augustine called her, usually heads the list but is accompanied by Johanna, Susanna, Salome, Mary the wife of Clopas, and others. Even the Samaritan woman at the well (Jn 4) is important not for her sexual impropriety, but for her preaching which brought a whole town to Jesus: "Many Samaritans from the city believed in him because of the women's testimony" (Jn 4:39). "Testimony" is a technical word signifying the word of apostolic witness. What is buried in this story is the memory of a successful missionary to the Samaritans, one who happens to be a woman with a checkered past. There are dozens of stories like this in the gospels, usually preached upon in a spiritualizing way, but actually containing the memory of women's discipleship in the ministry of Jesus.

5. Besides moving around with him in Galilee, the women disciples also followed Jesus up to Jerusalem. Every gospel makes it clear that they did not run and hide but stood by him in his hour of suffering. In fact, the only person named by all

four gospels as having stood by the cross is Mary Magdalene.
It is simply not true to say that all his disciples left him and
fled. In addition, some women disciples knew where the tomb
was, since they had helped to anoint the dead body of Jesus
and to bury him. Every gospel recounts the fact that it was
women disciples who discovered the tomb empty and first
received the news of the resurrection. In one gospel the message is proclaimed by an angel, but in the other three it is the
risen Lord himself who appears. Thus women were the first
recipients of a resurrection appearance. All four gospels show
that the women were commanded to "Go and tell"—that is,
they received the apostolic commission to preach in witness to
the risen Lord. All four gospels show that the women do so.
And they are not believed, since the male disciples think they
are telling idle tales (a point that has remained sadly true to
life!). Nevertheless, the testimony of the scriptures is that both
in his earthly life and risen life Jesus Christ included women in
his community, not as subordinates to males, but as equal
sisters to their brothers and, in the case of the resurrection
stories, even as those first entrusted.

6. In the early decades of the church there is strong evidence for a vigorous ministry of women as colleagues with
men. From the Acts of the Apostles and letters of Paul, we get
the picture of women as missionaries, preachers, teachers,
prophets, apostles, healers, speakers in tongues, leaders of
house churches. They are co-workers with Paul and the
others, gifted with all of the charisms which were given for the
building up of the church. Scholars are now trying to piece
together what forces brought this public ministry of women in
the early church to a diminished state.

7. As we have seen, virtually every reading of Jesus' death in
contemporary theology connects his end to his ministry. The
conflictual forces set up by his ministry brought him to his
death. In the feminist perspective, his inclusion of women
coequally in the reign of God was part of the offense he gave.

Furthermore, Jesus' crucifixion is seen as mounting a tremendous critique against patriarchy. On the cross Jesus symbolizes the exact opposite of male dominating power. Rather, on the cross power is poured out in self-sacrificing love. The cross is the *kenosis* of patriarchy. Looking at the cross, some feminists have reflected that sociologically it was probably better that the incarnation happened in a male human being; for if a woman had preached and enacted compassion and given the gift of self even unto death, the world would have shrugged—is not this what women are supposed to do anyway? But for a man to live and die this way in a world of male privilege is to challenge the patriarchal ideal of the dominating male at its root.

8. In the resurrection, the Spirit of God fills Jesus with new life and, present in the community in a new way, he becomes the cornerstone of the coming reign of God. His Spirit is poured out on all who believe, women equally with men. The early Christians adopted the initiation rite of baptism. Unlike the gender-specific Jewish ritual of circumcision, open only to males, baptism is inclusive since it is administered the same way to persons of both genders. Indicative of this, Paul's letter to the Galatians contains an early Christian baptismal hymn. As the newly baptized come up out of the water, all in white, wet robes, they sing, "Now there is no more Jew or Greek, slave or free, male or female, but all are one in Christ Jesus" (3:28). All divisions based on race, or class, or even gender are transcended in the oneness of the body of Christ. The power of the risen Christ becomes effective to the extent that this vision becomes reality in the community.

9. The early Christians named Jesus "Lord," "Christ," using images and titles taken from the Jewish and secular cultures with which they were familiar. One of the figures of the Jewish scriptures with which they identified him very early on (some think it was the first) was "Sophia," or Wisdom. This figure is a female personification of God in outreach to

the world. Sophia creates, redeems, establishes justice, protects the poor, teaches the mysteries of the world, and most especially gives life (see the Book of Wisdom). From Paul, who calls Jesus the wisdom of God (1 Cor 1:24), to John who models Jesus and his long discourses upon Sophia, wisdom christology offers the possibility of affirming the significance of Jesus Christ and of confessing even his divinity in a non-androcentric framework. As Sophia incarnate Jesus can be discerned as a coincidence of opposites in every respect: crucified yet glorified; God's own being yet made flesh; a man yet the prophet and very presence of Sophia herself. An ancient christological title is emerging with new dynamism in feminist reflection: Jesus-Sophia, or Jesus, the Wisdom of God.

In conclusion, feminist liberation christology has discovered Jesus as Liberator, not in a generic sense with regard to the poor but specifically with regard to women. He brings salvation through his life and Spirit, restoring women to full personal dignity in the reign of God, and inspiring their liberation from structures of domination and subordination. This is a challenging christology, as is every form of liberation theology. It signals a genuine Copernican revolution, this time not dethroning the earth in favor of the sun, but patriarchy in favor of a community of genuine mutuality. If it is good news to those oppressed, it can be a fearful thing to the oppressor. The call once again is for conversion of hearts, minds, and structures, so that the reign of God may take firmer hold in this world.

Readings

The best overview of feminist theology to date, including a chapter on the christological issue, is Anne Carr, *Transforming Grace: Christian Tradition and Women's Experience* (San Francisco: Harper & Row, 1988).

Much work has been done on the biblical testimony regarding Jesus and women. Elisabeth Schüssler Fiorenza, *In Memory of Her: A Feminist Theological Reconstruction of Christian Origins* (New York: Crossroad, 1983), discusses both the Sophia God of Jesus and Jesus' shaping of a community of the discipleship of equals; see also her "Word, Spirit and Power: Women in Early Christian Communities," in *Women of Spirit: Female Leadership in the Jewish and Christian Traditions*, Rosemary Radford Ruether and Eleanor McLaughlin, eds. (New York: Simon and Schuster, 1979), 29–70.

Other readable studies include Constance Parvey, "The Theology and Leadership of Women in the New Testament," *Religion and Sexism*, Rosemary Radford Ruether, ed. (New York: Simon and Schuster, 1974), 117–49; Elizabeth Carroll, "Women and Ministry," 660–86, and Raymond Brown, "Roles of Women in the Fourth Gospel," 688–99, in *Theological Studies* 36 (1975); Elisabeth Meier Tetlow, *Women and Ministry in the New Testament* (Lanham, MD: University Press of America, 1985); and Elisabeth Moltmann-Wendel, *The Women Around Jesus* (New York: Crossroad, 1982), which traces the trajectory of key women through the later tradition.

Reflections on these women and Jesus in a popular vein is offered by Rachel Conrad Wahlberg, *Jesus According to a Woman* and *Jesus and the Freed Woman* (New York: Paulist, 1975, 1978). Jesus' own attitude is highlighted by Leonard Swidler, "Jesus Was a Feminist," *New Catholic World* 214 (1971) 771–73.

The gender of Jesus and the way it has shaped christology is dealt with constructively by Rosemary Radford Ruether, "Christology and Feminism: Can a Male Saviour Save Women?" in *To Change the World: Christology and Cultural Criticism* (New York: Crossroad, 1981), and developed in her *Sexism and God-Talk: Toward a Feminist Theology* (Boston: Beacon, 1983); see also Sandra Schneiders, *Women and the Word: The Gender of God in the New Testament and the Spirituality of Women* (New York: Paulist, 1986). New images for christology are suggested by Patricia Wilson-Kastner, *Faith, Feminism and the Christ* (Philadelphia: Fortress, 1983); and Sallie McFague, *Models of God: Theology for an Ecological, Nuclear Age* (Philadelphia: Fortress, 1987).

8

God and the Cross

The world today is filled with suffering on a magnitude that boggles the imagination. It makes our time ripe for a discussion which is going on as a result of the new developments in christology. In the light of Jesus' history, of his ministry of great compassion toward people who were suffering, and especially of his degrading death on the cross, the question is urgently asked: "How does God relate to all of this suffering? Does God want it? Does God not want it, but permit it? Does it affect God too? Does God suffer when creatures whom God loves are suffering? Given our tormented world, can God love without in some way entering into suffering? What does christology, and especially the cross, have to say about how God relates to our situation?

On one side of the debate over this issue today are theologians who argue forcibly that God indeed suffers out of love, both in the death of Jesus on the cross and in the ongoing Auschwitzs of history. On the other side are those who argue just as strongly that it does no one any good if God suffers; rather, God is Being, pure livingness who makes all to be alive. When human beings whom God loves suffer, God is present with them, compassionately loving them through the suffering, desiring life for them, and acting to bring it about when human forces have played themselves out. Scripture and tradition form a rich background against which this theological discussion today is conducted. At the heart of it is an interpretation of Jesus Christ when viewed from the darkness of human pain and death.

Background

In both the Jewish and Christian scriptures, God is praised under two aspects. On the one hand, God is highly exalted, beyond the earth. No one has ever seen God or can imagine the divine being. No one knows God's thoughts or can control God in any way. This God is supremely free, having made the earth and everything in it. This God rules the earth and will bring all things to completion. From the point of view of God's transcendence, suffering cannot touch the divine being, for the Creator and Ruler of all things is supremely beyond its reach.

On the other hand, God is present in creation and dwells at the heart of all creatures—this is divine immanence in creation. As history develops God freely becomes very involved, caring about covenanted people, reprimanding them, trying one thing and then another to entice them to keep the covenant, getting the divine hands dirty (so to speak) with the troubles of those who suffer. When the Hebrews are enslaved in Egypt, for example, God calls upon Moses to lead the struggle for their release. Speaking to Moses from the burning bush, God says:

> I have seen the affliction of my people who are in Egypt; I have heard their cry because of their taskmasters; I know well what they are suffering; therefore I have come down to deliver them. (Ex 3:7–8)

Those verbs are filled with attentiveness and care: I have seen, heard, and known their pain; therefore I have come down. In fact, the word "know" (I *know* their sufferings) is the same as the word used in the book of Genesis when the first human beings are described: "Adam *knew* Eve his wife" (4:17). This is more than an intellectual knowing. It is an experiential knowing; they know one another bodily, so that a child is conceived. When God says "I know well what they are suffering," an interior personal kind of knowing is being talked about. God is involved in the sufferings of the enslaved people and is not distant, beyond the reach of their cries.

Many other examples of God's indwelling involvement exist in the scriptures. The prophet Hosea depicts God as saying about sinful people, "My heart turns over within me, my compassion grows warm and tender" (11:8). The word "compassion," when broken down to its root, means to suffer with, to feel with: God here is anything but cold and distant. In relation to insights of feminist theology, biblical scholars are pointing out that the root word for compassion in Hebrew is the same as the root word for woman's womb *(rhm)*. To say that God has compassion on us is literally to say that God has womb-love for us and loves us the way a mother loves the child of her womb. This love is costly. In the face of injustice the prophet Isaiah has God speak: "For a long time I have held my peace, I have kept still and restrained myself; but now I cry out like a woman in labor: I gasp and I pant" (42:14). Here we have not only a feminine image of God, but a very dramatic one, conveying the idea of God suffering in labor to bring forth the new creation. Along with God's free transcendence over history, the scriptures also bear the tradition of God's involvement with history, of God's somehow knowing what we suffer and suffering with us. It is basically the teaching of the pathos of God: the heart of God feels with us.

When Christianity in its missionary effort moved out into the Hellenistic world, it met a very different idea of God in classical Greek philosophy. God was characterized according to an ideal of immutable perfection beyond the world. The divine was thought of as an absolute, world-transcending, self-subsistent Being; an incomprehensible essence, with the attribute of impassibility, which means not being capable of suffering. To prevent God from being dependent on the world, any real relation between God and the world was denied. In eternal splendor, the Unmoved Mover reigned. This certainly protected the freedom and transcendence of God, but lost sight of the immanence of God. When the biblical idea of God involved with the world met this Greek idea of God not able to suffer, they entered into an uneasy marriage. By the time of the great theological systems of the Middle Ages, the doctrine of God was predominantly influenced by Greek understanding. In his *Summa Theologiae*, for example, Thomas Aquinas deals first with the one God and the divine nature *(De Deo Uno)*, describing attributes such as God's incapacity to suffer. Then he moves to the triune God, Father, Son, and Spirit *(De Deo Trino)*, followed finally by consideration of the God who became incarnate *(De Verbo Incarnato)*. Here it is said that on the cross the human nature of the Incarnate Word suffered. Human nature is limited and subject to suffering, so God in human nature is suffering. But is God as God in divine nature suffering on the cross? The answer is *no*, because there is already a definition in place which says that God cannot suffer. The suffering of Jesus belongs to God insofar as God has a human nature, but God's own being is not suffering.

This idea is very firmly in place in the Catholic theological tradition. It has been preached and taught, accompanied by a certain logic: by definition God cannot suffer because any such suffering in God would diminish divinity itself. Part of the difficulty today is that this idea, while evoking awe and admiration of God, also creates the impression that God is very far away from people who suffer and somehow does not feel for them. We imagine a cold and distant God who does not know from the inside what suffering is. In the twentieth century a gripping critique has been leveled at this idea of a God who cannot feel suffering. We are devastated by the experience of two world wars, of holocausts, of countless local wars, of apartheid, of torture as an instrument of state policy, of the threat of nuclear death, of starvation and hunger continuing right down to our own day. A God who is not affected by this in some way is a God not really worthy of our love. A God who is a spectator at all of this pain, who even permits it (for such is the classical view), this kind of God seems somehow morally intolerable to us. The whole modern movement of protest atheism springs from this reaction.

In response, there have been continuing moves in this century to rethink this question of God in relation to suffering. In the 1950's, for example, the French philosopher Jacques Maritain wrote: "We need to integrate suffering with God, for the idea of an insensitive and apathetic God is revolting to the masses." Even earlier the American process philosopher Alfred North Whitehead had worked out a theory of God as our great companion, "the fellow-sufferer who understands." The theologian who probably verbalized this most poignantly is Dietrich Bonhoeffer, who wrote from his cell in a Nazi prison that "only a suffering God can help." In that circumstance, his meditation drove him inexorably to the insight that God was in fact suffering in the suffering of the people in this war; furthermore, that it was the task of Christians to stand by God in his hour of grieving, and to participate with God in the suffering of this world. In recent decades this same question about God and suffering has come to special focus in contemporary christology as it ponders the crucifixion. How does God relate to the cross? The answer to this question connects directly to the wider question of how God relates to the suffering of the world.

God Suffers

The theological stance that argues for the suffering of God has been given its most eloquent articulation by Jürgen Molt-

mann, now a Reformed theologian who was himself a pris-
oner of war during World War II. In his book *The Crucified
God*, he depicts a God who literally suffers on the cross,
thereby identifying with the suffering of the whole world. His
argument begins by rejecting two options as deficient. On the
one hand, to say that God does not suffer is to make of God
an unfeeling monster in the face of so much suffering today.
On the other hand, it is not right either to say that God suffers
without any choice in the matter. This is the human, finite way
of suffering—it overtakes us and holds us in its grip. It is part
of our creatureliness that we cannot escape. But such a condition would not do justice to God who is supreme over all
the earth.

There is a third option, however, and this would be to say
that out of love God freely chooses to be affected by what
affects others, so that when people sin and suffer this influences the divine being. In this view, God suffers not out of a
deficiency of weakness in the divine nature, but out of the
fullness of love. Moltmann argues very strongly that if God
could not suffer in this way, then God would not be Love. For
it is of the essence of love to be affected by what is happening
to the one you love, and to suffer or rejoice as a result.

How does this work out in the event of the cross? Moltmann judges that the traditional interpretation that the Son
suffers in his human nature but not in divine nature is inadequate. Instead, he proposes thinking through the cross in
relation to the whole Trinity. Using an approach that might be
described as a narrative of doctrine, Moltmann describes the
scene. The world is in sin, and the Father in his great mercy
wishes to save us. Therefore, he freely hands his Son over to be
crucified, which will accomplish this salvation. This is a
theme in the scriptural letters of Paul: God delivered him up
for our sins. The Son willingly obeys his Father and allows
himself to be handed over: "Not my will but thine be done."
The cross, then, is an event between God and God; between

the Father giving up his Son and the Son willingly being given up. While Jesus suffers on the cross, both Father and Son are suffering, though in different ways. The Father is suffering the grief of the loss of his Son. The Son is suffering the loss of his own life, and even more deeply the abandonment by his Father: "My God, my God, why have you forsaken me?" The two of them are deep in suffering, and this penetrates the very being of God. In a very literal sense, God is suffering.

Yet while each is suffering the loss of the other, they have never been so deeply united in one love. In their common loving will to save the world, regardless of the cost, what is revealed is the Holy Spirit, who is the Love of the Father and Son. At Jesus' death his Spirit, God's Love, is let loose on the world. The Love between Father and Son is released into creation and begins to bring about redemption.

The cross opens a pathway for all the suffering of the world to be taken into the very being of God. God is now so tied into history through his freely given Love on the cross that the pain of the world is admitted into himself. There, the power of divine Love heals, changes, saves it. By a kind of alchemy of Love, all the negativity of suffering is touched by God and transformed into the victory of life. Thus, Moltmann will say not only that God is in history, but history with all of its uproars is in God; not only God in Auschwitz, but Auschwitz in God. Through the dialectic of being and nonbeing in God, the negativity of history is brought to a new and just reconciliation. In fact, *only* if all disaster is within God can God affect salvation. Otherwise, it is still apart from divine power and is not changed.

Moltmann is obviously depending here upon a pattern of thinking associated with dialectical philosophy as worked out by Hegel, namely, the idea that history proceeds according to the dynamic of thesis, antithesis, synthesis. Thesis: There is suffering on the cross and in the world. Antithesis: This suffering affects God and even appears to overcome him (Jesus dies). Synthesis: God transforms the suffering into life (the resurrection in the Spirit). This theology of the trinitarian transactions in the event of the cross works itself out as a divine dialectic grappling with the history of the world.

Moltmann presents a shattering example of this theology of the cross and the suffering of God by quoting a passage from Eli Wiesel's novel *Night*. A survivor of the concentration camps of the Second World War, Wiesel was given the Nobel Peace Prize for his work as a witness to the memory of the dead so that this will never happen again. One passage of this novel, based on firsthand experience, describes:

> The SS hanged two Jewish men and a youth in front of the whole camp. The men died quickly, but the death throes of the youth lasted for half an hour. "Where is God? Where is he?" someone asked behind me. As the youth still hung in torment in the noose after a long time, I heard the man call again, "Where is God now?" And I heard a voice within myself answer, "Where is he? He is here, he is hanging there on the gallows . . ."

Any other answer would be blasphemy, judges Moltmann. There cannot be any other Christian answer to the question of this torment. To speak here of a God who did not feel the suffering of his creatures would be really to make God a demon, an unfeeling, unthinking, uncaring, unhelpful monster. Where is God? He is there on the cross, there on the gallows, there where anyone suffers. God is there, suffering with the beloved creature. Moltmann has given us the idea of a very alive and compassionate God who overcomes evil on a personal and cosmic scale through his own self-involvement.

God Is Compassionately Present

A different but no less compelling way of theologizing about the cross and God's suffering is being developed by

Edward Schillebeeckx. This theologian is intensely concerned with the excess of suffering in the world and the question it raises for faith. True, he writes, there is some suffering that is beneficial in human life. It comes in the normal course of events and helps to mature us, to develop our character, to open our heart in compassion for others who suffer. Some suffering saves us from superficiality and shallowness. But there is too much other suffering in the world, suffering that does not create character but destroys it. There is an excessive suffering of the innocent, the undeserved suffering of millions of people at the hands of other people who gain advantage from this. This suffering is like a surd in history. It does not make sense; it wrecks every theory constructed to explain it. This is the deep mystery of evil at work in the world.

Rather than see this uproar of history as entering into the very being of God, however, Schillebeeckx has developed an approach more within the lines of the classic Catholic tradition. He is basically a Thomist, adhering to the school of thought that describes God as Pure Act, Being Itself, whose very essence is to be. Negativity is the opposite of being and can gain no foothold in God. More pastorally phrased, God is pure positivity, in whom there is no shadow. God is pure Life, unalloyed Love, desiring only life and not death for his creatures. And yet there is evil in the world. As transacted in Jesus, God gives an unqualified Yes to the good of humanity, freely willing that the evil which destroys his beloved creation shall be overcome.

From this perspective, Schillebeeckx disagrees point for point with Moltmann's reading of the cross. First of all, the Father does not hand Jesus over or deliver him up to suffering. The way we have thought and preached about this has made God into a kind of sadist. What sort of human father would hand his child over to such torture? To say that God willed Jesus to suffer makes God less good than a normal human being would be. Historically speaking, Jesus was condemned to death unjustly, a victim of human sinfulness and rejection.

To say that God handed him over is to blame God for what should be laid at the doorstep of human injustice. Rather, God wills life and not death, joy and not suffering, both for Jesus and for everyone else.

In addition, the cross is not an event between God and God, a tearing apart between the Father and the Son. Rather, the cross reveals instead the tension between God and sinful humanity; it is the index of what is opposed to God in the world. Nor does the Father suffer the loss of his Son. In Schillebeeckx's interpretation of the cross, God as pure positivity enters into compassionate solidarity with Jesus on the cross, keeping faith with him, not abandoning him. God is present in the mode of absence. He keeps vigil until human freedom has played itself out and Jesus is destroyed. Then God overcomes the evil of death through the eschatological act of resurrection, conquering and undoing the negativity wrought by human sinfulness. Then it can be confessed that God was present all along—under the conditions of finitude and history. So vital is the resurrection as a sign of God's fidelity to Jesus that Schillebeeckx insists the cross by itself cannot save. In itself it is evil in its destruction of Jesus. It is sinful, and only Jesus' love and fidelity, along with God's overcoming the negativity of the cross in the resurrection, effect our salvation. In one sense, he would say, we are saved not by the cross but despite it.

Finally, Schillebeeckx argues, suffering does not enter the being of God. Would this not glorify evil and give it a value and a predominant place which it does not deserve? Furthermore, how is it good news for us if God too is suffering? How can God save if God too needs to be rescued, if we are all in the same boat together? Suffering "contaminates" the being of God with the very sickness from which we need to be freed. Rather, what happens at the cross and consequently at all other suffering moments is that God, who is the absolute foe of evil, enters into compassionate solidarity with the suffering one in order to save. As pure positivity, God persists in the fullness of Being, of Love, while forming a community of interest with Jesus. God is with him in the midst of his suffering, near but silent, bending over him to gift him with life. The evil of this world, with all its power, is weaker than God, the compassionate One who enters into solidarity with the sufferer and, ultimately, saves.

Thus, in contrast to Moltmann's narrative, Schillebeeckx would contend that God does not suffer, nor does suffering enter the being of God. Against traditional Thomism, however, he would also contend that God does not want or even "permit" human beings to suffer. His stance would be for a different concept altogether: for God who, while not suffering, strongly resists evil and is in solidarity with those who suffer, overcoming that suffering in a powerful movement of loving compassion. In addition, God's compassionate presence is mediated through the human presence and action of believers, who resist injustice as sacraments of God's own saving will. Unlike the dialectical thinking of Moltmann, this approach is more in keeping with the analogical imagination of the Catholic tradition. It preserves God's impassibility (or quality of not suffering) as a sign of God's transcendence and freedom. But this is preserved only as the reverse side of divine compassion, which renders God powerfully sympathetic toward the pain of the world and discloses God ultimately as the Living One. At this point in his discussion of the problem Schillebeeckx halts, overwhelmed by the reality of which he speaks. Theoretically we cannot explain this: the mystery of evil, and the depths of God's essential positivity, compassionate over suffering and victorious over evil.

Outcome

Both Moltmann and Schillebeeckx, who are themselves representative of a much wider theological discussion about suffering, present us with a God who is much more involved in the pain of history than the God of classical Christian theism. They are both interested in showing that the victims of history, those who suffer excessively, are in the end lifted up by the living God. Whichever philosophic system one prefers, or even if one prefers neither, it is evident that thinking God from the cross turns us away from an apathetic vision of God, from a God distant from human suffering, to one who is powerfully involved in suffering and moves to overcome it.

Out of this kind of reflection has come yet another new title for Jesus Christ. He may be called Jesus, the Compassion of God. In the tradition, other divine qualities have been used to name Jesus—he is Wisdom, the Word, the Truth, and so on. In our time, with our awareness of the compassionate nature of his ministry, and with our reading of the cross as the event where God's solidarity with those who suffer came to an unsurpassed focus, we can say of Jesus that the divine quality of the Compassion of God became incarnate in him.

This way of thinking about God also makes clear the call to the community of disciples: we are united with God in Jesus by being in compassionate solidarity with those who suffer. If God is there, resisting evil and willing life wherever people are being damaged, then the followers of Jesus must enter into the same solidarity. There is a traditional axiom which claims that to live a good ethical life one must "do good and avoid evil." The emphasis shifts today, slightly but very dramatically, to make us realize that this is not enough. In fact, it can end up being a shirking of responsibility. For in the light of the compassion of God revealed in Jesus, we must "do good and resist evil." There is a call to the Christian conscience here not to hide our face from evil, not to walk around it, or pretend it is not there; but to face its massiveness in spite of our feelings of powerlessness or insignificance and to become involved in transforming it. Suffering people are the privileged place where the God of compassion is to be found.

Readings

The views on the cross explained in this chapter are found in Jürgen Moltmann, *The Crucified God: The Cross of Christ as the Foundation and Criticism of Christian Theology* (New York: Harper & Row, 1974); and in Edward Schillebeeckx's *Jesus* and *Christ* books (see chap. 4, above). A good survey of Protestant thinkers including Moltmann on this subject is Warren Mc-Williams, *The Passion of God: Divine Suffering in Contemporary Protestant Theology* (Macon, GA: Mercer University Press, 1985). Lucien Richard, *A Kenotic Christology: In the Humanity of Jesus the Christ, the Compassion of Our God* (Lanham, MD: University of America Press, 1982), works out the issue in a contemporary Catholic fashion; so too does Monika Hellwig, *Jesus, the Compassion of God* (Wilmington, DL: Glazier, 1985). An excellent and readable treatment of God's involvement in the abandonment of Jesus is Gérard Rossé, *The Cry of Jesus on the Cross: A Biblical and Theological Study* (New York: Paulist, 1987). Leonardo Boff presents meditations on the cross from a liberation perspective in *Passion of Christ, Passion of the World* (Maryknoll, NY: Orbis, 1987). The relation of the cross to prayer is explored by Sebastian Moore, *The Crucified Jesus Is No Stranger* (New York: Seabury, 1977).

9

Salvation of the Whole World

The turn to the subject in modern thought, that is, to the personal and the historical, has been correlated in christology with new understandings of the genuine humanity of Jesus Christ and of his unique, concrete, personal history. The modern turn to the negative likewise has been appropriated within christology by new understandings of Jesus' liberating relation to the poor and oppressed, to women within patriarchy, and to persons who suffer injustice in the maelstrom of history. Each interaction between these contemporary currents and central affirmations of the faith tradition has shaped a new burst of insights. These have rolled into Christian consciousness like waves breaking on the beach, roughly sequential but in the end mixing together to bring in the tide.

The turn to the global in modern consciousness is the generating force behind the newest wave forming in christology. Who do we say that Jesus Christ is in the face of the whole world which knows itself to be truly one world? This question began shaping christological interest in the late 1970's and 1980's and will continue to do so into the twenty-first century. What is at stake is the universality of Jesus Christ both with regards to all people of the earth and to all creatures of the earth, the whole cosmos itself.

All People

From the beginning the Christian proclamation about
Jesus Christ, crucified and risen, was possessed of a universal
thrust. In short order early missionaries moved outward from
Palestine in an effort to reach the whole world. The good
news of God's drawing near in liberating compassion to persons dispossessed by sin was too good to be restricted to any
one group. The resurrection of Jesus signaled a living future
not only for Jewish believers but for the whole human race.
Late in the first century this insight was made explicit by one
Christian letter writer: God our Savior "desires all people to
be saved and to come to the knowledge of the truth" (1 Tim
2:5).

While the scriptures vigorously affirm the universality of
God's saving will, it fell to later thinkers to explain how this is
accomplished. A particular difficulty arises in view of the fact
that not all people are baptized, not all people even want to be
baptized. Are the unbaptized saved? If they are not, does this
not frustrate God's universal saving will? And if they are, how
does this square with the confession that God saves the
human race through Jesus Christ? For it would seem that
persons not baptized are not related to Jesus Christ and do
not follow his way. In the centuries of Christendom when the
church was a big church in the little world of medieval Europe, the problem was not pressing. In Christian perception
Jews and infidels were thought to be beyond the pale of God's
saving mercy in Christ, mercy which was not abundantly
available even to Christians who lived in fear of their own
damnation.

In our own day, however, such a view has faded, both in the
popular imagination and in official teaching. The Second
Vatican Council reaffirmed the scriptural affirmation that salvation is a possibility for every person. In ways known only to
God's own self, the offer of salvation is made to all:

All this holds true not only for Christians, but for all people of good will in whose hearts grace works in an unseen way. For since Christ died for all people, and since the ultimate vocation of the human race is in fact one, and divine, we ought to believe that the Holy Spirit in a manner known only to God offers to every human being the possibility of being associated with this paschal mystery. (*Church in the Modern World,* 22)

Consequent to this a new question has arisen in christology. How are we to reconcile the belief that all people are offered the possibility of salvation with the belief that salvation comes through Jesus Christ, the one mediator between God and human beings? At least three positions can be identified in the current theological debate about salvation in Christ and the peoples of the world. While the majority of Catholic theologians since the council have held in various ways to the second position, each of the others has its own adherents.

1. One theological camp stakes out the position that Jesus Christ is constitutive for salvation and that this is to be interpreted in an exclusive sense.

Thinkers of this perspective hold to the confession that Jesus Christ is the only true Savior, there being no other name by which we can be saved. Saving faith in Christ is usually explicit, however, so that only those who actually confess Jesus Christ can be saved. The axiom that "outside the church there is no salvation," taken out of its historical context in the third century and applied literally, leads to the conclusion that people who are not Christian are saved, if at all, by way of exception. The church then becomes the zone of the saved versus the wider world of the unsaved. There is thus an exclusivity to the salvation won by Jesus Christ, since it is enjoyed mainly by Christians.

Held too rigidly, this position leads to undermining God's salvific plan for all people. Even in the patristic era, the axiom "outside the church there is no salvation" was not taken absolutely literally. Justin, for example, envisioned the Logos, the Word of God, scattering seeds of truth and goodness through the world. The pagan religions and Greek philosophy could then be seen not as divorced from God but as preparations for the gospel, as forerunners of Christ. With baptism by water setting apart those who were in the church from those who were not, Augustine developed the idea of two other kinds of baptism which could save: baptism of blood, for those who intended to be Christian but were martyred before they could actually receive the baptismal water; and baptism of desire, for those who wished to be Christian but died before they were explicitly received into the church.

Again, in face of the medieval focus on Christians who were thought to be in the majority in the world, theologians such as Thomas Aquinas opened the door to a wider participation in God's grace. He wrote, for example:

> If someone grows up in the forest or among wild animals, then it belongs to God's providence to provide such a person with the necessaries for salvation, provided the person places no obstacles in the way. If someone who grows up in these circumstances follows the lead of natural reason in seeking the good and refusing evil, it must be held that God will actually reveal to him by an internal inspiration those things which he needs to believe.

When the so-called Age of Exploration in the sixteenth century brought Europeans into contact with vast numbers of people who were not Christian, theology took further cautions to prevent whole tribes from being thought outside of God's saving mercy. This led to ideas such as invincible ignorance (they are not guilty of not knowing about Christ) and implicit desire (they desire to do the will of God, and would be baptized if they knew about it) coming into prominence.

While the salvation of those "outside" was always held to be a possibility, however, the prevailing idea for centuries was that salvation on a wide scale for those outside was not all that likely. There was a certain pessimism about this, related to how difficult it was felt to be for Catholics themselves to work out their salvation even inside the church. The church was the ordinary way of salvation, and if someone was saved outside of its visible boundaries, that was extraordinary. The missionary work of the church was motivated by this conviction. It was urgently necessary to preach and baptize, or the salvation of whole peoples would be in danger. This first stance, especially characteristic of the church from the Middle Ages up to the twentieth century, holds that Christ is essential for salvation; but his saving power is not universally available, apart from some few exceptions.

2. A second position likewise holds that Christ is constitutive for salvation but, unlike the first, argues that this is to be interpreted in an inclusive sense.

By mid-twentieth century the church found itself in a new situation. Owing to communications and ease of travel multiple encounters with the world religions were taking place, and the results were sobering. After two thousand years of Christian mission approximately one-third of the world is Christian with the remainder belonging to the other world religions or even to no religion at all. China, for example, is a country of one billion people with no discernible religion. In addition, the world religions themselves show no signs of disappearing. They are experiencing an upsurge in vitality that makes it unlikely that a great number of their members will be converted to Christianity. There is the further discovery that all of the world religions uphold the religious and moral dimensions of human life—justice and peace—in the midst of a materialistic, warlike, and even atheistic world.

Even before the Second Vatican Council all of these elements: realization of the sheer numbers of people "outside" the church, the continuing vitality of the religions, appreciation of their spiritual wisdom, making common cause for human good, had opened up a new situation for reflection. In its *Declaration on the Relation of the Church to Non-Christian Religions (Nostra Aetate)* the council took notice of this development and even encouraged it. The teaching of this declaration is strongly universal. It begins with the affirmation that there is only one God who created all people. All human beings are made in the divine image and have a basic orientation to God. God's will to save is universal and comes to focus in Christ who died in order to save all. Whatever is true and holy in the world's religions is a reflection of the one divine light which enlightens the whole world. Encounter and dialogue are to replace avoidance and condemnation. As for individual persons, God in ways hidden in divine mystery inspires each one's conscience and enables each one to be faithful to grace.

A certain optimism of salvation becomes part of the teaching of the church through this council. Christ's grace reaches more people and operates in more diverse ways than we might have suspected. Jesus Christ is essential for salvation, but his saving power is given a more inclusive thrust. This has given theology a new question to wrestle with, namely, how can we confess Jesus Christ as the only Savior and still hold that many who do not confess him are saved? If everyone has the possibility to be saved, even within their own religion, what does that do to the universality of Jesus Christ? The effort in christology since the council has been to envision how this "works."

The most far-reaching thesis so far has been put forward by Karl Rahner, who has influenced a whole generation of thinkers on this question. His thinking builds on the belief that there is only one God, who designed one saving mystery in Jesus Christ. All people, therefore, who are trying to do the will of God, listening to their own conscience and trying to lead a good moral life, are actually being guided by the saving grace of Christ (there is no other). They are saying Yes to Christ, although they may not know it. As those who explicitly know and praise Jesus Christ, members of the church can recognize in other people the same saving grace at work. Therefore, we may call these people "anonymous Christians," for they are responding to the grace of Christ although they do not name him.

In this view, Christian mission is not a matter of announcing something that is foreign to peoples' lives. Betraying his geographical centeredness in central Europe, Rahner says that proclaiming Christ is not similar to informing people that the continent of Australia exists! Rather, it is a matter of bringing to consciousness and making explicit something that is already known implicitly. Like Paul at Athens, the missionary announces the name of the God who has been worshiped without a name. The missionary calls upon people to become aware of who they already are in Jesus Christ.

For those who do not hear this call and stay within the religion of their culture, that very religion can be a means by which grace is mediated. The positive structures of a religion are seen as the means through which saving grace, which in the Catholic view is never unmediated, becomes effective; the religions in their truth and holiness may be legitimate ways of salvation. Thus, Hindus may be saved not despite their religion but precisely by being good Hindus. Rahner would say that there is a time limit to this, and that once people have heard the truth of the gospel in their own existence, then it is mandatory upon them to follow Christ in a more explicit way. But until that moment, the one salvation brought by Christ may be mediated to them anonymously, through the religion in which they were born and brought up.

Rahner has been strongly criticized for his theory of the anonymous Christian, both from the right and the left. Hans Urs von Balthasar, a more conservative theologian, has said that the phrase "anonymous Christian" is like "wooden iron," a contradiction in terms; for by definition a Christian is someone whose name is publicly linked to the name of Jesus in baptism, and who clearly walks the path of discipleship. On the other hand, Hans Küng has found the theory imperialistic and conducive of a sense of superiority, with Christians saying to other people: we know who you are better than you know yourselves. True dialogue becomes impossible if one side starts out knowing all the truth. In rebuttal of this last criticism, Rahner recounted the moment when he was asked how he would feel if a Buddhist told him that he was an anonymous Buddhist. He replied that he would be honored, for the Buddhist would be crediting him with participating in the highest truth as it was known in Buddhism.

Other theologians have worked out different approaches. Küng's own thesis sees Christ as the light of the world, whose brightness is reflected through the historical ministry of Jesus and the ongoing witness of the church in the world. Whoever is saved is saved through the impact of this paradigmatic historical example and its ongoing influence. Aloysius Pieris (Sri Lanka) takes note of the similarity between Jesus' historical life and the lives of poverty and asceticism lived by so many Asian peoples. What connects Jesus, who was Asian, and Asian peoples today is not some supernatural entity but the red thread of suffering and quiet attentiveness to the presence of God. In these concrete, existential forms a solidarity between Jesus and Asian people is forged, a solidarity which is saving.

The writings of Raimundo Panikkar provide an exceptionally clear example of an inclusivist position. Born in India of Christian and Hindu parents, Panikkar's experience as a priest and a theologian has led him to appreciate the insights of both faith traditions. In *The Unknown Christ of Hinduism,* he puts forth the understanding that the Word did indeed become flesh in Jesus—but not only there. The Word is capable of more than one incarnation and can be thought to have been embodied in Eastern culture as well as within Western history. Thus, the Word (Christ) is present within saving figures of Hinduism, bringing the way of salvation to millions who otherwise might not be found by grace. The mystery of God with us is more diverse than we have imagined.

Most influential, though, continues to be Rahner's understanding. In the storm of debate he has said many times by now that we can drop the term "anonymous Christian"; he is not wedded to it. But the reality to which that term points is vital. Everyone who is saved is somehow involved in the saving mystery of the one God in Christ, whatever the external and concrete circumstances of their life. Christians are the historically visible vanguard of this salvation working itself out in history. Knowing Jesus Christ explicitly, they are like morning light on the mountains which signals to those in the valley that the night is over. But they are not the light above judging the darkness below; for the light is coming to shine universally on all people, and to guide them to salvation.

3. A third, more debatable proposal holds that Jesus Christ is not constitutive for salvation, but rather is normative.

More recently, theologians who have been actively engaged in dialogue with thinkers of the world religions, who have actually sat down at table with them and tried to dialogue, have been developing the notion that Jesus Christ is not constitutive for the salvation of all people, but that he is extremely important. For those who believe in him, he is a norm for human behavior and even for the revelation of God. For those who do not, he functions to measure and correct whatever in their religion may be deficient. Thus, he is normative in a universal way. But Jesus Christ is not constitutive for salvation because other savior figures directly related to their own cultures reveal the divine mystery in a way that is also normative. In other words, Jesus Christ alone does not exhaust the possibilities of being savior. Buddha or Krishna also have a role, and may endorse and uphold values that Christians may tend to overlook. Compared with the other two positions, this stance is not so much christocentric as it is theocentric, or centered on God who is at the heart of all the religions.

This position emphasizes that there is one God, who saves in various ways; Jesus Christ is the Way for Christians, but other ways exist for the millions of people in cultures with different religions. Theologically a great deal needs to be worked out in this position's coherence with the saving role of Jesus Christ as affirmed in the tradition, if this position is to win a place as a viable understanding for the future. Still, as Susan Sontag has noted in another connection, there are ways of thinking that we do not yet know about. Christian understanding of the universal relevance of Jesus Christ will continue to be shaped by ongoing experiences of encounter and dialogue in an increasingly small world.

Whatever position one fields on the question of Christ's universality, the ferment surrounding the question in the last thirty years has led theology to be much more optimistic about the salvation of all peoples in the world. We are more ready to grant that God can reach people in whatever circumstances they find themselves and bring them to salvation. The patristic idea credited to Origen that all are in fact saved *(apocatastasis)* is once again being studied. While the operation of human freedom does not really allow us to assert definitively that all are saved, because there is always the possibility that some persons may freely choose to sin and not repent, we recognize more clearly today that at least God wishes everyone to be saved. While we may not be sure that everyone is saved, at least we can *hope* that everyone is. As Schillebeeckx sees it, everyone has at least given a cup of water and in thus loving their neighbor has honored Christ. The universality of Jesus Christ gives ground for the hope that the power of God triumphs over sin in the life of every person, whether they are members of the visible church or not.

In a meditation on Holy Saturday Hans Urs von Balthasar has created a striking parable of the mystery of universal

salvation. After his crucifixion and death Jesus descends into
hell. This is not just *Sheol,* the shadowy place of the dead, or
the anteroom where the just women and men of the Old
Testament were awaiting entrance into heaven. It is the hell of
eternal damnation, the hell of hardened sinners. The crucified
Christ enters this hell quietly and is simply there with the
damned, gazing on them with unutterable love. When they see
the profound love of God for them, love that self-emptied even
to the cross leaving wounds and scars that will never disappear, the heart of even the most hardened sinner just melts. If
Christ had entered into hell triumphantly, or had given them
one last chance to repent "or else," in macho fashion, resistance would have been fierce. But who can withstand such love
that is willing to go to the dregs of annihilation for castoff
persons accounted of no worth? In the end through the cross
the love of God wins what it has been after all along, namely,
the return love of the beloved creatures, even those who had
shut themselves off. At least, says von Balthasar, that is what
we may hope.

The Whole Cosmos

Christian theology of the last few centuries concentrated so
intensely on redemption of the human race that for the most
part it lost sight of the great scriptural and patristic theme that
Jesus Christ is also the Savior of the whole world, of the
natural world and all of its creatures. The focus was on
deliverance from personal sin which while certainly appropri-
ate was only partial insofar as the theme of creation in
christology was neglected. Circumstances are now leading to
a rediscovery of this important dimension of redemption. An
ecological crisis is afflicting the world in many quarters. Our
life-supporting systems of fresh water, clean air, fertile soil,
and protective ozone layer are being ruined by toxic effluents,
pollutants, acids, all the poisonous waste products of modern

society. Just as serious, through the destruction of habitats we
are rapidly destroying hundreds of life forms, species which
took thousands of years to develop and which the earth will
never see again. Magnificent animals and complex plants are
disappearing from the earth. In an unthinkable way the nuclear buildup holds over the head of every living creature the
threat of total extinction, the death of birth itself.

What does Jesus Christ have to do with all of this? Is he not
the Redeemer of the whole world? How does creation become
an intrinsic part of our christological confession? Once again,
theologians are searching the treasures of the tradition and
discovering valuable insights.

The story of Jesus is recalled once again to empower conversion from the greed and disrespect which lead people to
rape the earth for profit. Jesus' vision of the reign of God
includes wholeness and *shalom* for all creatures, even the least
important in the present hierarchy of values, the nonhuman.
God's peace links all creatures in a community of life and
stands against exploitation even of the least powerful. In the
new heaven and the new earth, every created thing will have its
own integrity in relationships of mutuality and interdepen-
dence. For those who follow Jesus, not self-interest but respect
for all of God's creatures is what should hold sway.

In addition, Jesus' example inculcates an attitude of wonder
and appreciation for the natural world. He could read the
signs of the sky and what they told about the coming weather;
he knew of sunsets, of the lilies of the field, of fig trees, of
mother hens, of seeds, and of the fruits of the earth. As many
of his parables and sayings reveal, he was in tune with the
beatitudes of the earth, seeing in them a reflection of aspects of
God who sends rain on the just and unjust. Exploitation and
destruction of the earth and its creatures are foreign to this
kind of attitude.

The crucified Jesus was raised from the dead by the power
of the Spirit of God whom we confess in the creed as "the

Lord and Giver of Life." Jesus Christ lives now by the Spirit and pours forth this Spirit to renew human hearts and even the face of the earth. Once again, renewed awareness of the theme of the Spirit in christology is opening the way to care for all creatures.

The Spirit is the shaper of the new creation, dwelling at the heart of all things and working to redeem them. In his letter to the Romans Paul expresses this very poetically. All creation has been subjected to futility, but it is waiting with eager longing for the glory that is to come. It will be set free from its bondage to decay and share in the glorious liberty of the children of God. Meanwhile, along with human beings, creation is groaning and in labor until the gift of the Spirit be given (8:18–23). In other words, it is not just human beings who are saved. We are of a piece with all creation, sharing with all creatures a common destiny. The new heaven and the new earth for which we hope includes the renewal of the whole universe. The dynamic power effecting this redemption at the end and weaving webs of community between all creatures in the interim is the Holy Spirit of the risen Christ. In this understanding, both spirituality and ethics direct us toward responsible stewardship of the earth.

The theme that Christ is at the center of creation is also a powerful biblical rediscovery of our time. He is the Word through whom all things were made; as the firstborn of creation he is the one in whom all things hold together (Jn 1:3; Col 1:15–20). If he is the Alpha, he is also the Omega of creation: the first and last word which reconciles all things in the peace of God. The ancient eastern doctrine of recapitulation is relevant here. Just as all things fell apart in Adam, so too the reverse happens in Christ. All things find their right harmony and fulfillment in him. We may be more familiar with the thinking of Teilhard de Chardin in our own century, who also gave this idea new life. The earth, the natural world, is not divorced from God—most religious persons would say that. But neither is it divorced from Christ, since in Jesus Christ's incarnation God and the world, the infinite and the finite, divine and creature, are brought into intimate contact. Jesus Christ is the summit of creation, the Omega Point, and evolutionary history is but the straining of all creatures toward him as their goal. This kind of christology offers a powerful deterrent to exploitation of the earth for the earth is pervaded with significance within the divine milieu.

Celebration of sabbath may be the best way to inculcate a christology which promotes respect for the earth. The founding story of this day in Genesis (1:31–2:3) portrays God in an endearing way as resting on the seventh day, after looking over everything just created and finding it very good. Finished with the work of creation, God takes delight in all that is made. A nonutilitarian, reposeful presence of the Creator pervades all that has been created—a clue to the final redemption. In imitation of God, the Israelites who were led out of slavery were commanded to observe the sabbath as a celebration of their liberation from slave labor. No one was to do any work, not even the animals; but all were to delight in the presence of the Creator within the good creation and offer praise. Under the impact of the resurrection of Christ, Christian celebration of this day moved from the seventh to the first day of the week. Now creation is contemplated through the prism of the risen Christ, whose risen body is bonded with the whole earth as a sign of the promise of the new creation already beginning.

In no way is this concern for ecological justice separated from the desire for justice and peace among human beings. Making one vital connection between them, liberation theology has encouraged the celebration of the sabbath by oppressed people as a subversive activity. Taking time out from the grimness of daily life, people gather to sing and praise, to share and be joyful. It is a sign of resistance, for in effect they are saying that their spirits are not crushed; hope is alive that someday they will be free of this oppression. To yield to despair is to let the oppressor win. To come together to celebrate, rest, delight, sense the presence of God in all things, and taste the promise offered by the resurrection of Christ is to engage in profound opposition to destructive forces.

In our day the humanocentrism of much of christology is expanding toward a cosmic vision of the significance of Jesus Christ. Both the example of Jesus and Spirit christologies point the way toward a new, urgently needed appreciation of the universality of reconciliation at work in the world through Christ. The promise of that redemption is meant for all the peoples of the world and for the whole cosmos itself.

Readings

Excellent overviews of the various positions regarding the universality of Christ are Peter Schineller, "Christ and Church: A Spectrum of Views," *Theological Studies* 37 (1976) 545–66; Lucien Richard, *What Are They Saying about the Uniqueness of Christ and World Religions?* (New York: Paulist, 1981); and more broadly, Paul Knitter, *No Other Name? A Critical Survey of Christian Attitudes toward the World Religions* (Maryknoll, NY: Orbis, 1985). Knitter himself argues for a theocentric christology. Theological reflections on the subject abound in Gerald Anderson and Thomas Stransky, eds., *Christ's Lordship and Religious Pluralism* (Maryknoll, NY: Orbis, 1981); and in John Hick and Brian Hebblethwaite, eds., *Christianity and Other Religions* (Philadephia: Fortress, 1981).

Karl Rahner's position is laid out in "Christianity and the Non-Christian Religions," *Theological Investigations* 5:115–34; "Anonymous Christianity and the Missionary Task of the Church," *Theological Investigations* 12 (New York: Seabury, 1974), 161–78; and is especially clear in "The One Christ and the Universality of Salvation," *Theological Investigations* 16 (New York: Seabury, 1979), 199–224. Hans Küng's stance is taken in "The World Religions in God's Plan of Salvation," *Christian Revelation and World Religions,*

Joseph Neuner, ed. (London: Burns and Oates, 1967), 25–66; Aloysius Pieris begins the Asian exploration in "Speaking of the Son of God in Non-Christian Cultures, e.g., Asia," *Jesus, Son of God?* Edward Schillebeeckx and J.B. Metz, eds. (New York: Seabury, 1982), 65–70; and continues with "The Buddha and the Christ: Mediators of Liberation," *The Myth of Christian Uniqueness,* John Hick and Paul Knitter, eds. (Maryknoll, NY: Orbis, 1988). Raimundo Panikkar's stance is worked out in *The Unknown Christ of Hinduism* (rev. ed., Maryknoll, NY: Orbis, 1981), and *The Intrareligious Dialogue* (New York: Paulist, 1978).

A particularly fascinating aspect of this issue is the relation of the Jewish people to Jesus Christ today. This is explored by John Pawlikowski, *Christ in the Light of the Christian-Jewish Dialogue* (New York: Paulist, 1982); Eugene Borowitz, *Contemporary Christologies: A Jewish Response* (New York: Paulist, 1980); and Pinchas Lapide and Ulrich Luz, *Jesus in Two Perspectives: A Jewish-Christian Dialogue* (Minneapolis: Augsburg, 1985).

Hans Urs von Balthasar's insights on the paschal mystery appear in his *Life out of Death: Meditations on the Easter Mystery* (Philadelphia: Fortress, 1985), and in *The von Balthasar Reader,* Medard Kehl and Werner Löser, eds. (New York: Crossroad, 1982), 147–56.

The need for theology to develop a global consciousness in this age of ecological disasters is powerfully stressed by Sallie McFague, *Models of God* (above, chap. 7); also by Rosemary Radford Ruether, "Ecology and Human Liberation: A Conflict between the Theology of History and the Theology of Nature?" *To Change the World: Christology and Cultural Criticism* (above, chap. 7). The cosmic Christ in relation to the universe is praised by Teilhard de Chardin, *Hymn of the Universe* (New York: Harper & Row, 1965), and explained further by Christopher Mooney, *Teilhard de Chardin and the Mystery of Christ* (Garden City, NY: Doubleday, 1968). An overview of this theme focusing on scripture and the Greek Fathers is George Maloney, *The Cosmic Christ: From Paul to Teilhard* (New York: Sheed and Ward, 1968).

Afterword
A Living Tradition—Toward the Future

"Who do you say that I am?" We have traced the development of contemporary christology with the metaphor of successive waves of renewal breaking on the beach. In our day theology has retrieved the genuine humanity of Jesus Christ, remembered his concrete story, realized his liberating power for the poor and oppressed, and probed the breadth and depth of his saving power for the peoples of the world and the whole earth itself. If I may be allowed a prediction, the next wave to rise and roll into the church's consciousness will be that of non-western christologies, as the young and growing churches of Africa, Asia, and India formulate their own answer to the christological question in words and concepts taken from their own cultures. We are in a period of christological ferment unmatched since the first century. Like the first-century church reflected in the New Testament we once again have a pluralism of christologies or different ways of formulating Jesus Christ's significance and identity while remaining united in the confession of the one faith. Like the Christians of the first century, we too are being called to write the good news in an idiom suitable to our time and place. Like them we are living disciples and need to be about the never-finished business of confessing Jesus Christ in a pilgrim church. Out of our own experience of salvation, our own telling of the story, our own praxis and prayer, we must name Jesus Christ again and claim him again for our own people, so that a living christology will be handed on to the next generation into the twenty-first century.

Index

147